A BOOK OF
ENGLISH PROSE

5·27·82

A BOOK OF
ENGLISH PROSE
1700-1914

EDITED BY

ERIC PARTRIDGE

BOOKS FOR LIBRARIES PRESS
FREEPORT, NEW YORK

STANDARD BOOK NUMBER:

8369-5385-1

LIBRARY OF CONGRESS CATALOG CARD NUMBER:

73-119942

PRINTED IN THE UNITED STATES OF AMERICA

CONTENTS

4 *Contents*

INTRODUCTION

The limits set by the years 1700–1914 have their reasons. In 1700 began the essentially modern use of prose ; Dryden, who died in that year, had been in many ways an exponent of a modern prose, but, if we set him beside Addison and Defoe, we perceive that the ease and naturalness of the essayist and the novelist differentiate them from such writers as Cowley, Dryden and Temple, make them participators in the intellectual democracy of the eighteenth and nineteenth centuries, and cause their writings to become links in a chain sympathetic to modern readers. The modern spirit was feeling its way during the Restoration period, and the prose displays a certain tentativeness. The anthology ends in spirit at the date of August 3, 1914, for the editor feels that after August 4, something new entered into the hearts and minds, the moral and intellectual composition of English writers : just as literature changed after the French Revolution and the Napoleonic Wars, so, but much more profoundly (he believes), literature is in the process of changing after the Great War and the concomitant as well as subsequent unrest. To pass beyond the year 1914 is to take into our survey a period that we may not understand for many years.

The exact title of this volume should be " A Book of Typically English Prose, 1700–1914," where " typically " would imply the presence of those qualities which we regard as national. The editor has aimed not at producing an anthology of narrow or nationalistic tendency, but at giving examples (for the scope prevents him from calling it an anthology) of such prose as we

5

associate naturally with English writers and at excluding
certain other kinds which, although they may be
genuinely racy of the soil, do not seem to be so charac-
teristically native as the clear, vigorous, manly, frank,
healthy, adventurous, homely prose of men like Defoe.
At least one of those qualities will be found in every
piece, but they do not exclude polish, as we see in
Addison ; they admit the intellectuality of Gibbon
because of his clarity and chastened vigour, while they
exclude Newman and Pater for their alienation from
what we might term an essentially native standard ;
the beautiful is present, but it must not be morbid
or recondite ; sentimentality and emotionalism are
debarred (hence the omission of a Richardson or a
Sterne) ; of criticism there is only one example, and
that because it consists of a tribute to our greatest
genius,—for some reason, the critical, despite such
fine exponents of that art as Arnold or Dowden, does not
fall in the list of those kinds of writing which one would
spontaneously declare English, and so even Matthew
Arnold is passed by ; and while philosophical, theological and political works have flourished in England,
they would clash with the general purpose of the editor,
who wishes to present a group of writings at once
interesting and literary and to illustrate the more
vigorous, obvious virtues of prose. In short, he desires
to set forth a summary illustrative record of such
qualities as have endowed English prose with life and
endurance rather than of such as make it an intellectual
or magnificently sensuous expression of doubly excep-
tional personalities. In the cultivated prose of an
Addison there is energy, in the vigorous prose of a Swift
there is culture, and in both there is life, the zest of
creation. Admiration for the prose of Berkeley,
Coleridge, and Morley should not blind us to the fact
that, although such writers have enriched the content
of our prose literature, they have (along with a Newman
or a Wilde) done less to continue its vigour and to provide
its sap than Defoe and Trelawny with their masculine

prose of adventure, than Burns and Hugh Miller with
their homely native genius. Writers so diverse as
Scott, Dickens Thackeray, Meredith and Hardy,
despite the complexity of the fourth, are all healthy
and native to the soil. The eloquence and beauty
of Burke and Ruskin have an immediacy of appeal
absent from the specifically imaginative prose of De
Quincey ; moreover, Burke and Ruskin saw that prose
thrives best if it is kept distinct from poetry, while
De Quincey frequently lapses into " poetic prose,"
which, beautiful and suggestive, yet tends to relax
the salutary check of metre in poetry and to rob prose
of its precision.

Of the normal characteristics at any period, many
will be found in the writing of history, because, if
history necessarily precludes the manner of novel and
essay, it does give free play to clarity, vigour, and frank-
ness, which, indeed, it demands. Three different
kinds of historical composition are to be seen in Gibbon,
Macaulay, and Froude, but how good they are ! Like
Buffon, Gibbon shows what can be done by organic
composition if there is energy at command, and it is
in energy that the English writer surpasses the French :
Macaulay expresses himself in prose admirably adapted
to narrative and to characterization, to rapid summary
as to detail,—in short, Taine was right when he said
that if Macaulay lost favour in England, so much the
worse for England, because his somewhat circum-
scribed character was, in certain most important
respects, typical and brilliantly representative of the
English intellect : and Froude so combines force,
picturesqueness, ease and clarity that his pages breathe
forth the very man.

In history, those three writers are truly representative
of the qualities that they possess so pre-eminently. The
novel has been exemplified by Fielding and the most
significant men of the Nineteenth Century ; the extracts
are meant to illustrate the straightforward, not too
psychological, achievements. The short story, a modern

development, requires an early example, Hawthorne, and a late, to indicate the change that has come over the genre. (Hawthorne, by the way, and Poe are included because the former was very English and the latter is most significant in the history of our prose.) The essay speaks for itself from the mouths of Addison (whose art, in the general essay, remained unsurpassed in his century), Goldsmith (the forerunner of Lamb in the personal and whimsical), Lamb himself, his contemporaries Hazlitt and Leigh Hunt (who close a splendid efflorescence of the essay), and as typical of the kind much later, Stevenson. Several less distinguished divisions call for suitable representatives in Landor and De Quincey, Miller and Trelawny, while eloquence has been entrusted to one man, Burke. Space, however, prevents the original, native Jane Austen and the fascinating Sir Richard Burton from being included.

Lest it should be inferred that, in these various kinds, only narrative or something analogous thereto have found a place, the present writer hastens to say that the qualities of vigour, manliness, clarity, healthiness and the like may well inform a description or a reflection, a preface or an epilogue. As a healthy life and a healthy outlook do much for national existence, so corresponding qualities in the writers make inestimably for the permanency of our literature : and it is especially in prose that we look for energy, good health and sanity, which may characterize even so fervent a devotee of beauty as Ruskin.

Within these, rather limits than limitations, the editor believes that he has introduced much of that variety which the wits claim as the sauce, and certain philosophers as the source of life, but he wishes to add that several noticeable omissions have been made in subservience to an ideal of selection.

ERIC PARTRIDGE.

May, 1926.

A BOOK OF ENGLISH PROSE
(1700-1914)

Stage Lions

There is nothing that of late years has afforded
matter of greater amusement to the town than Signior
Nicolini's combat with a lion in the Haymarket, which
has been very often exhibited to the general satisfaction
of most of the nobility and gentry in the kingdom of
Great Britain. Upon the first rumour of this intended
combat, it was confidently affirmed, and is still believed
by many in both galleries, that there would be a tame
lion sent from the Tower every opera night, in order
to be killed by Hydaspes ; this report, though altogether
groundless, so universally prevailed in the upper regions
of the playhouse, that some of the most refined politicians in those parts of the audience gave it out in
whisper, that the lion was a cousin-german of the tiger
who made his appearance in King William's days, and
that the stage would be supplied with lions at the
public expense, during the whole session. Many likewise
were the conjectures of the treatment which this lion
was to meet with from the hands of Signior Nicolini :
some supposed that he was to subdue him in recitativo,
as Orpheus used to serve the wild beasts in his time,
and afterwards to knock him on the head ; some fancied

that the lion would not pretend to lay his paws upon
the hero, by reason of the received opinion, that a lion
will not hurt a virgin : several, who pretended to have
seen the opera in Italy, had informed their friends,
that the lion was to act a part in High-Dutch, and
roar twice or thrice to a thorough-bass, before he fell
at the feet of Hydaspes. To clear up a matter that
was so variously reported, I have made it my business
to examine whether this pretended lion is really the
savage he appears to be, or only a counterfeit.

But before I communicate my discoveries, I must
acquaint the reader, that upon my walking behind the
scenes last winter, as I was thinking on something
else, I accidentally justled against a monstrous animal
that extremely startled me, and upon my nearer survey
of it, appeared to be a lion rampant. The lion seeing me
very much surprised, told me, in a gentle voice, that I
might come by him if I pleased : "For," says he,
"I do not intend to hurt anybody." I thanked him
very kindly, and passed by him. And in a little time
after saw him leap upon the stage, and act his part
with very great applause. It has been observed by
several, that the lion has changed his manner of acting
twice or thrice since his first appearance ; which will
not seem strange, when I acquaint my reader that the
lion has been changed upon the audience three several
times. The first lion was a candle-snuffer, who, being a
fellow of a testy, choleric temper, over-did his part,
and would not suffer himself to be killed so easily as he
ought to have done ; besides, it was observed of him,
that he grew more surly every time he came out of the
lion, and having dropt some words in ordinary conversation, as if he had not fought his best, and that he suffered
himself to be thrown upon his back in the scuffle, and
that he would wrestle with Mr. Nicolini for what he
pleased, out of his lion's skin, it was thought proper

to discard him : and it is verily believed, to this day,
that had he been brought upon the stage another time,
he would certainly have done mischief. Besides, it was
objected against the first lion, that he reared himself
so high upon his hinder paws, and walked in so erect
a posture, that he looked more like an old man than
a lion.

The second lion was a tailor by trade, who belonged
to the playhouse, and had the character of a mild and
peaceable man in his profession. If the former was
too furious, this was too sheepish for his part ; inso-
much, that after a short modest walk upon the stage,
he would fall at the first touch of Hydaspes, without
grappling with him, and giving him an opportunity of
showing his variety of Italian trips. It is said, indeed,
that he once gave him a rip in his flesh-coloured doublet ;
but this was only to make work for himself, in his
private character of a tailor. I must not omit that it
was this second lion who treated me with so much
humanity behind the scenes.

The acting lion at present is, as I am informed, a
country gentleman, who does it for his diversion, but
desires his name may be concealed. He says, very
handsomely, in his own excuse, that he does not act
for gain ; that he indulges an innocent pleasure in it ;
and that it is better to pass away an evening in this
manner than in gaming and drinking : but at the
same time says, with a very agreeable raillery upon
himself, that if his name should be known, the ill-
natured world might call him, "the ass in the lion's
skin." This gentleman's temper is made out of such a
happy mixture of the mild and the choleric, that he
outdoes both his predecessors, and has drawn together
greater audiences than have been known in the memory
of man.

I must not conclude my narrative, without taking

notice of a groundless report that has been raised to
a gentleman's disadvantage, of whom I must declare
myself an admirer; namely, that Signior Nicolini
and the lion have been seen sitting peaceably by one
another, and smoking a pipe together behind the scenes;
by which their common enemies would insinuate,
that it is but a sham combat which they represent upon
the stage: but upon inquiry I find, that if any such
correspondence has passed between them, it was not
till the combat was over, when the lion was to be looked
upon as dead, according to the received rules of the
drama. Besides, this is what is practised every day
in Westminster Hall, where nothing is more usual than to
see a couple of lawyers, who have been tearing each other
to pieces in the court, embracing one another as soon as
they are out of it.

I would not be thought, in any part of this relation,
to reflect upon Signior Nicolini, who in acting this
part only complies with the wretched taste of his
audience; he knows very well, that the lion has many
more admirers than himself; as they say of the famous
equestrian statue on the Pont Neuf at Paris, that more
people go to see the horse than the king who sits upon
it. On the contrary, it gives me a just indignation to
see a person whose action gives new majesty to kings,
resolution to heroes, and softness to lovers, thus sinking
from the greatness of his behaviour, and degraded into
the character of the London Prentice. I have often
wished, that our tragedians would copy after this great
master in action. Could they make the same use of
their arms and legs, and inform their faces with as
significant looks and passions, how glorious would
an English tragedy appear with that action which
is capable of giving a dignity to the forced
thoughts, cold conceits, and unnatural expressions of an
Italian opera! In the mean time, I have related this

combat of the lion, to show what are at present the reigning entertainments of the politer part of Great Britain.

Joseph Addison (1672-1719).

A Journey across Africa

In the very first entrance of the waste, we were exceedingly discouraged ; for we found the sand so deep, and it scalded our feet so much with the heat, that, after we had, as I may call it, waded rather than walked through it about seven or eight miles, we were all heartily tired and faint—even the very negroes lay down and panted, like creatures that had been pushed beyond their strength.

Here we found the difference of lodging greatly injurious to us, for, as before, we always made us huts to sleep under, which covered us from the night air, which is particularly unwholesome in those hot countries ; but we had here no shelter, no lodging, after so hard a march, for here were no trees—no, not a shrub near us—and, which was still more frightful, towards night we began to hear the wolves howl, the lions bellow, and a great many wild asses braying, and other ugly noises, which we did not understand.

Upon this we reflected upon our indiscretion—that we had not, at least, brought poles or stakes in our hands, with which we might have, as it were, palisadoed ourselves in for the night, and so we might have slept secure, whatever other inconveniences we suffered. However we found a way at last, to relieve ourselves a little. For, first, we set up the lances and bows we had, and endeavoured to bring the tops of them as near to one another as we could, and so hung our coats

on the top of them, which made us a kind of sorry
tent. The leopard's skin, and a few other skins we
had put together, made us a tolerable covering, and
thus we lay down to sleep, and slept very heartily too
for the first night, setting, however, a good watch,
being two of our own men with their fusees, whom we
relieved in an hour at first, and two hours afterwards ;
and it was very well we did this, for they found the
wilderness swarmed with raging creatures of all kinds,
some of which came directly up to the very enclosure
of our tent. But our sentinels were ordered not to
alarm us with firing in the night, but to flash in the
pan at them, which they did, and found it effectual,
for the creatures went off always as soon as they saw
it, perhaps with some noise or howling, and pursued
such other game as they were upon.

If we were tired with the day's travel, we were all as
much tired with the night's lodging : but our black
prince told us in the morning he would give us some
counsel, and indeed it was very good counsel. He told us
we should be all killed, if we went on this journey, and
through this desert, without some covering for us at
night ; so he advised us to march back again to a little
river side, where we lay the night before, and stay there
till we could make us houses, as he called them, to
carry with us to lodge in every night. As he began
a little to understand our speech, and we very well to
understand his signs, we easily knew what he meant,
and that we should there make mats (for we remembered
that we saw a great deal of matting, or bass there,
that the natives made mats of) ; I say, that we should
make large mats there for covering our huts or tents
to lodge in at night.

We all approved this advice, and immediately resolved
to go back that one day's journey, resolving, though
we carried less provisions, we would carry mats with

us, to cover us in the night. Some of the nimblest
of us got back to the river with more ease than we had
travelled it but the day before ; but, as we were not
in haste, the rest made a halt, encamped another night,
and came to us the next day.

In our return of this day's journey, our men, that
made two days of it, met with a very surprising thing,
that gave them some reason to be careful how they parted
company again. The case was this. The second day
in the morning, before they had gone half a mile, looking
behind them, they saw a vast cloud of sand or dust
rise in the air, as we see sometimes in the roads in
summer, when it is very dusty, and a large drove of
cattle are coming, only very much greater ; and they
could easily perceive that it came after them ; and it
came on faster than they went from it. The cloud of
sand was so great that they could not see what it was
that raised it ; and concluded that it was some army
of enemies that pursued them ; but then considering
that they came from the vast uninhabited wilderness,
they knew it was impossible any nation or people that
way should have intelligence of them, or the way of
their march ; and therefore, if it was an army, it must
be of such as they were travelling that way by accident.
On the other hand, as they knew that there were no
horse in the country, and that they came on so fast,
they concluded that it must be some vast collection
of wild beasts, perhaps making to the hill country
for food or water, and that they should be all devoured
or trampled under foot by their multitude.

Upon this thought they very prudently observed
which way the cloud seemed to point, and they turned
a little out of the way to the north, supposing it might
pass by them. When they were about a quarter
of a mile they halted to see what it might be. One of
the negroes, a nimbler fellow than the rest, went back

a little, and came in a few minutes, running as fast as the heavy sand would allow ; and by signs gave them to know that it was a great herd or drove of elephants.

As it was a sight our men had never seen, they were desirous to see it, and yet a little uneasy at the danger too ; for though an elephant is a heavy, unwieldy creature, yet in the deep sand, which was nothing at all to them, they marched at a great rate, and would soon have tired our people, if they had had far to go, and had been pursued by them.

Our gunner was with them, and had a great mind to have gone close up to one of the outermost of them, and to have clapped his piece to his ear, and to have fired into him, because he had been told no shot would penetrate them ; but they all dissuaded him, lest, upon the noise, they should all turn upon and pursue us : so he was reasoned out of it, and let them pass, which, in our people's circumstances, was certainly the right way.

They were between twenty and thirty in number, but prodigious great ones ; and though they often showed our men that they saw them, yet they did not turn out of their way, or take any other notice of them, than, as we may say, just to look at them. We that were before saw the cloud of dust they raised, but we thought it had been our own caravan, and so took no notice ; but as they bent their course one point of the compass, or thereabouts, to the southward of the east, and we went due east, they passed by us at some little distance ; so that we did not see them, or know anything of them, till evening, when our men came to us, and gave us this account of them. However, this was a useful experiment for our future conduct in passing the desert, as you shall hear in its place.

We were now upon our work, and our black prince was head surveyor, for he was an excellent mat-maker him-

self, and all his men understood it ; so that they soon
made us near a hundred mats ; and as every man, I
mean of the negroes, carried one, it was no manner
of load, and we did not carry an ounce of provisions the
less. The greatest burthen was to carry six long poles,
besides some shorter stakes ; but the negroes made an
advantage of that, for carrying them between two,
they made the luggage of provisions which they had to
carry so much the lighter, binding it upon two poles,
and made three couple of them. As soon as we saw
this we made a little advantage of it too ; for having
three or four bags, called bottles (I mean skins or bladders
to carry water), more than the men could carry, we
got them filled, and carried them this way, which was
a day's water and more, for our journey.

Having now ended our work, made our mats, and fully
recruited our stores of things necessary, and having made
us abundance of small ropes and matting for ordinary
use, as we might have occasion, we set forward again,
having interrupted our journey eight days in all, upon
this affair. To our great comfort, the night before we
set out there fell a very violent shower of rain, the
effects of which we found in the sand ; though the
one day dried the surface as much as before, yet it was
harder at bottom, not so heavy, and was cooler to our
feet, by which means we marched, as we reckoned,
about fourteen miles instead of seven, and with much
more ease.

When we came to encamp we had all things ready, for
we had fitted our tent, and set it up for trial, where we
made it ; so that, in less than an hour, we had a large
tent raised, with an inner and outer apartment, and
two entrances. In one we lay ourselves, in the other
our negroes, having light pleasant mats over us, and
others at the same time under us. Also, we had a
little place without all for our buffaloes, for they deserved

B

our care, being very useful to us, besides carrying forage and water for themselves. Their forage was a root, which our black prince directed us to find, not much unlike a parsnip, very moist and nourishing, of which there was plenty wherever we came, this horrid desert excepted.

When we came the next morning to decamp, our negroes took down the tent, and pulled up the stakes ; and all was in motion in as little time as it was set up. In this posture we marched eight days, and yet could see no end, no change of our prospect, but all looking as wild and dismal as at the beginning. If there was any alteration, it was that the sand was nowhere so deep and heavy as it was the first three days. This we thought might be because, for six months of the year, the winds blowing west (as for the other six they blew constantly east), the sand was driven violently to the side of the desert where we set out, where the mountains lying very high, the easterly monsoons, when they blew, had not the same power to drive it back again ; and this was confirmed by our finding the like depth of sand on the farthest extent of the desert to the west.

It was the ninth day of our travel in this wilderness when we came to the view of a great lake of water ; and you may be sure this was a particular satisfaction to us, because we had not water left for above two or three days more, at our shortest allowance ; I mean, allowing water for our return, if we had been put to the necessity of it. Our water had served us two days longer than expected, our buffaloes having found, for two or three days, a kind of herb like a broad flat thistle, though without any prickle, spreading on the ground, and growing in the sand, which they eat freely of, and which supplied them for drink as well as forage.

The next day, which was the tenth from our setting

out, we came to the edge of this lake, and, happily for us, we came to it at the south point of it ; so we passed by it, and travelled three days by the side of it, which was a great comfort to us, because it lightened our burthen, there being no need to carry water when we had it in view. And yet, though here was so much water, we found but very little alteration in the desert ; no trees, no grass or herbage, except that thistle, as I called it, and two or three more plants, which we did not understand, of which the desert began to be pretty full.

But as we were refreshed with the neighbourhood of this lake of water, so we were now gotten among a prodigious number of ravenous inhabitants, the like whereof, it is most certain, the eye of man never saw : for, as I firmly believe, that never man, nor any body of men, passed this desert since the flood, so I believe there is not the like collection of fierce, ravenous, and devouring creatures in the world ; I mean, not in any particular place.

For a day's journey before we came to this lake, and all the three days we were passing by it, and for six or seven days' march after it, the ground was scattered with elephants' teeth in such a number as is incredible ; and, as some of them may have lain there for some hundreds of years, so, seeing the substance of them scarce ever decays, they may lie there, for aught I know, to the end of time. The size of some of them is, it seems, to those to whom I have reported it, as incredible as the number ; and I can assure you there were several so heavy as the strongest man among us could not lift. As to number, I question not there are enough to load a thousand sail of the biggest ships in the world, by which I may be understood to mean that the quantity is not to be conceived of ; seeing that as they lasted in view for above eighty miles travelling, so they might continue as far to the right hand, and to the left as far, and many times as far, for aught we knew ; for it seems the number of elephants hereabouts is prodigiously great. In one place in particular we saw the head of an elephant, with several teeth in it, but one of the biggest that ever I saw ; the flesh was consumed to be sure many hundred years before, and all the other bones ; but three of our strongest men could not lift this skull and teeth ; the great tooth, I believe, weighed at least three hundredweight ; and this was particularly remarkable to me, for I observed the whole skull was as good ivory as the teeth ;[1] and, I believe, altogether weighed at least six hundredweight ; and though I do not know but, by the same rule, all the bones of the elephant may be ivory, yet I think there is a just objection against it, from the example before me, that then all the other bones of this elephant would have been there as well as the head.

I proposed to our gunner, that, seeing we had travelled now fourteen days without intermission, and that we had water here for our refreshment, and no want of food yet, nor any fear of it, we should rest our people a little, and see, at the same time, if, perhaps, we might kill some creatures that were proper for food. The gunner, who had more forecast of that kind than I had, agreed to the proposal, and added, why might we not try to catch some fish out of the lake ? The first thing we had before us was to try if we could make any hooks, and this indeed put our artificer to his trumps ; however, with some labour and difficulty, he did it, and we catched fresh fish of several kinds. How they came there none but He that made the lake, and all the world, knows ; for, to be sure, no human hands ever put any in there, or pulled any out before.

We not only catched enough for our present refresh-

[1] A traveller's tale !

ment, but we dried several large fishes, of kinds which
I cannot describe, in the sun, by which we lengthened
out our provisions considerably ; for the heat of the
sun dried them so effectually without salt that they
were perfectly cured, dry, and hard in one day's time.

We rested ourselves here five days ; during which time
we had abundance of pleasant adventures with the wild
creatures, too many to relate. One of them was very
particular, which was a chase between a she-lion, or
lioness, and a large deer ; and, though the deer is
naturally a very nimble creature, and she flew by us
like the wind, having, perhaps, about three hundred
yards the start of the lion, yet we found the lion, by
her strength, and the goodness of her lungs, got ground
of her. They passed by us within about a quarter of
a mile, and we had a view of them a great way, when,
having given them over, we were surprised about an
hour after to see them come thundering back again
on the other side of us, and then the lion was within
thirty or forty yards of her ; and both straining to
the extremity of their speed, when the deer, coming
to the lake, plunged into the water, and swam for her
life, as she had before run for it.

The lioness plunged in after her, and swam a little
way, but came back again ; and, when she was got
upon the land, she set up the most hideous roar that
ever I heard in my life, as if done in the rage of having
lost her prey.

We walked out morning and evening constantly ;
the middle of the day we refreshed ourselves under our
tent ; but one morning early we saw another chase,
which more nearly concerned us than the other ; for
our black prince, walking by the side of the lake, was
set upon by a vast great crocodile, which came out of
the lake upon him ; and though he was very light of
foot, yet it was as much as he could do to get away ;

he fled amain to us, and the truth is we did not know
what to do, for we were told no bullet would enter her ;
and we found it so at first, for though three of our men
fired at her, yet she did not mind them ; but my friend
the gunner, a venturous fellow, of a bold heart, and
great presence of mind, went up so near as to thrust
the muzzle of his piece into her mouth, and fired, but
let his piece fall, and ran for it the very moment he had
fired it ; the creature raged a great while, and spent
its fury upon the gun, making marks on the very iron
with her teeth, but after some time fainted and died.

Our negroes spread the banks of the lake all this while
for game, and at length killed us three deer, one of
them very large, the other two very small. There was
water-fowl also in the lake, but we never came near
enough to them to shoot any ; and, as for the desert,
we saw no fowls anywhere in it, but at the lake.

We likewise killed two or three civet cats ; but their
flesh is the worst of carrion. We saw abundance of
elephants at a distance, and observed they always
go in very good company—that is to say, abundance
of them together, and always extended in a fair line of
battle ; and this, they say, is the way they defend
themselves from their enemies ; for, if lions or tigers,
wolves, or any creatures, attack them, they being drawn
up in a line, sometimes reaching five or six miles in
length, whatever comes in their way is sure to be trod
under foot, or beaten in pieces with their trunks, or
lifted up in the air with their trunks : so that if a
hundred lions or tigers were coming along, if they meet
a line of elephants, they will always fly back till they
see room to pass by to the right hand or to the left ;
and if they did not, it would be impossible for one of
them to escape ; for the elephant, though a heavy
creature, is yet so dexterous and nimble with his trunk,
that he will not fail to lift up the heaviest lion, or any

other wild creature, and throw him up in the air quite over his back, and then trample him to death with his feet. We saw several lines of battle thus ; we saw one so long, that indeed there was no end of it to be seen, and, I believe, there might be two thousand elephants in a row or line. They are not beasts of prey, but live upon the herbage of the field, as an ox does ; and it is said, that though they are so great a creature, yet that a smaller quantity of forage supplies one of them than will suffice a horse.

The numbers of this kind of creature that are in those parts are inconceivable, as may be gathered from the prodigious quantity of teeth, which, as I said, we saw in this vast desert ; and indeed we saw a hundred of them to one of any other kinds.

One evening we were very much surprised ; we were most of us laid down on our mats to sleep, when our watch came running in among us, being frightened with the sudden roaring of some lions just by them, which, it seems, they had not seen, the night being dark, till they were just upon them. There was, as it proved, an old lion and his whole family, for there was the lioness and three young lions, beside the old king, who was a monstrous great one : one of the young ones, who were good, large, well-grown ones too, leaped up upon one of our negroes, who stood sentinel, before he saw him, at which he was heartily frightened, cried out, and ran into the tent : our other man, who had a gun, had not presence of mind at first to shoot him, but struck him with the butt-end of his piece, which made him whine a little, and then growl at him fearfully ; but the fellow retired, and, we being all alarmed, three of our men snatched up their guns, ran to the tent door, where they saw the great old lion by the fire of his eyes, and first fired at him, but, we supposed, missed him, or at least did not kill him ; for they went all off, but raised a most hideous roar, which, as if they had called for help, brought down a prodigious number of lions, and other furious creatures, we know not what, about them, for we could not see them ; but there was a noise and yelling, and howling, and all sort of such wilderness music on every side of us, as if all the beasts of the desert were assembled to devour us.

We asked our black prince what we should do with them. Me go, says he, and fright them all. So he snatches up two or three of the worst of our mats, and, getting one of our men to strike some fire, he hangs the mat up at the end of a pole, and set it on fire, and it blazed abroad a good while, at which the creatures all moved off, for we heard them roar, and make their bellowing noise at a great distance. Well, says our gunner, if that will do, we need not burn our mats, which are our beds to lay under us, and our tilting to cover us. Let me alone, says he. So he comes back into our tent, and falls to making some artificial fire-works, and the like ; and he gave our sentinels some to be ready at hand upon occasion, and particularly he placed a great piece of wildfire upon the same pole that the mat had been tied to, and set it on fire, and that burnt there so long that all the wild creatures left us for that time.

However, we began to be weary of such company, and, to get rid of them, we set forward again two days sooner than we intended. We found now that, though the desert did not end, nor could we see any appearance of it, yet that the earth was pretty full of green stuff of one sort or another, so that our cattle had no want ; and, secondly, that there were several little rivers which ran into the lake, and, so long as the country continued low, we found water sufficient, which eased us very much in our carriage, and we went on still sixteen days more without yet coming to any appearance of better soil. After this we found the country rise a little, and by that we perceived that the water would fail us, so for fear of the worst, we filled our bladder bottles with water. We found the country rising gradually thus for three days continually, when, on the sudden, we perceived, that though we had mounted up insensibly, yet that we were on the top of a very high ridge of hills, though not such as at first.

Daniel Defoe (1661–1731).

From " Captain Singleton."

The Capture of a Fleet

The empire of Blefuscu is an island, situated to the north-east side of Lilliput, from whence it is parted only by a channel of eight hundred yards wide. I had not yet seen it, and upon this notice of an intended invasion, I avoided appearing on that side of the coast, for fear of being discovered by some of the enemy's ships, who had received no intelligence of me, all intercourse between the two empires having been strictly forbidden during the war, upon pain of death, and an embargo laid by our Emperor upon all vessels whatsoever. I communicated to his Majesty a project I had formed of seizing the enemy's whole fleet : which, as our scouts assured us, lay at anchor in the harbour ready to sail with the first fair wind. I consulted the most experienced seamen upon the depth of the channel, which they had often plumbed, who told me, that in the middle, at high water, it was seventy glumgluffs deep, which is about six feet of European measure ; and the rest of it fifty glum-gluffs at most. I walked towards the north-east coast, over against Blefuscu ; where, lying down behind a hillock, I took out my small perspective glass, and

viewed the enemy's fleet at anchor, consisting of about
fifty men-of-war, and a great number of transports :
I then came back to my house, and gave order (for which
I had a warrant) for a great quantity of the strongest
cable and bars of iron. The cable was about as thick
as pack-thread, and the bars of the length and size of a
knitting needle. I trebled the cable to make it stronger,
and, for the same reason, I twisted three of the iron bars
together, binding the extremities into a hook. Having
thus fixed fifty hooks to as many cables, I went back
to the north-east coast, and putting off my coat, shoes,
and stockings, walked into the sea, in my leathern jerkin,
about an hour before high water. I waded with what
haste I could, and swam in the middle about thirty
yards, till I felt ground ; I arrived to the fleet in less
than half an hour. The enemy was so frighted when
they saw me, that they leaped out of their ships, and
swam to shore, where there could not be fewer than
thirty thousand souls. I then took my tackling, and,
fastening a hook to the hole at the prow of each, I tied
all the cords together at the end. While I was thus
employed, the enemy discharged several thousand
arrows, many of which stuck in my hands and face :
and, besides the excessive smart, gave me much disturb-
ance in my work. My greatest apprehension was for
mine eyes, which I should have infallibly lost, if I
had not suddenly thought of an expedient. I kept
among other little necessaries a pair of spectacles in
a private pocket, which, as I observed before, had
escaped the Emperor's searchers. These I took out
and fastened as strongly as I could upon my nose, and,
thus armed, went on boldly with my work in spite of
the enemy's arrows, many of which struck against the
glasses of my spectacles, but without any other effect,
farther than a little to discompose them. I had now
fastened all the hooks, and, taking the knot in my hand,

began to pull, but not a ship would stir, for they were all too fast held by their anchors, so that the boldest part of my enterprise remained. I therefore let go the cord, and leaving the hooks fixed to the ships, I resolutely cut with my knife the cables that fastened the anchors, receiving above two hundred shots in my face and hands ; then I took up the knotted end of the cables to which my hooks were tied, and with great ease drew fifty of the enemy's largest men-of-war after me.

The Blefuscudians, who had not the least imagination of what I intended, were at first confounded with astonishment. They had seen me cut the cables, and thought my design was only to let the ships run adrift, or fall foul on each other : but when they perceived the whole fleet moving in order, and saw me pulling at the end, they set up such a scream of grief and despair, that it is almost impossible to describe or conceive. When I had got out of danger, I stopt a while to pick out the arrows that stuck in my hands and face : and rubbed on some of the same ointment that was given me at my first arrival, as I have formerly mentioned. I then took off my spectacles, and, waiting about an hour till the tide was a little fallen, I waded through the middle with my cargo, and arrived safe at the royal port of Lilliput.

The Emperor and his whole court stood on the shore expecting the issue of this great adventure. They saw the ships move forward in a large half-moon, but could not discern me, who was up to my breast in water. When I advanced to the middle of the channel, they were yet in more pain, because I was under water to my neck. The Emperor concluded me to be drowned, and that the enemy's fleet was approaching in a hostile manner : but he was soon eased of his fears, for the channel growing shallower every step I made, I came in a short time within hearing, and, holding up the end of the cable by which the fleet was fastened, I cried in a

loud voice, Long live the most puissant Emperor of
Lilliput ! This great prince received me at my landing
with all possible encomiums, and created me a nardac
upon the spot, which is the highest title of honour
among them.

Jonathan Swift (1667–1745).

From " Gulliver's Travels."

The Beginning of a Great Novel

THE INTRODUCTION TO THE WORK, OR BILL OF FARE TO THE FEAST

An author ought to consider himself, not as a gentleman who gives a private or eleemosynary treat, but
rather as one who keeps a public ordinary, at which
all persons are welcome for their money. In the former
case, it is well known that the entertainer provides
what fare he pleases ; and though this should be very
indifferent, and utterly disagreeable to the taste of
his company, they must not find any fault ; nay, on
the contrary, good breeding forces them outwardly to
approve and to commend whatever is set before them.
Now the contrary of this happens to the master of an
ordinary. Men who pay for what they eat will insist
on gratifying their palates, however nice and whimsical
these may prove ; and if everything is not agreeable
to their taste, will challenge a right to censure, to abuse,
and to d—n their dinner without controul.

To prevent, therefore, giving offence to their customers
by any such disappointment, it hath been usual with the
honest and well-meaning host to provide a bill of fare
which all persons may peruse at their first entrance
into the house ; and having thence acquainted them-

selves with the entertainment which they may expect, may either stay and regale with what is provided for them, or may depart to some other ordinary better accommodated to their taste.

As we do not disdain to borrow wit or wisdom from any man who is capable of lending us either, we have condescended to take a hint from these honest victuallers, and shall prefix not only a general bill of fare to our whole entertainment, but shall likewise give the reader particular bills to every course which is to be served up in this and the ensuing volumes.

The provision, then, which we have here made is no other than *Human Nature*. Nor do I fear that my sensible reader, though most luxurious in his taste, will start, cavil, or be offended, because I have named but one article. The tortoise—as the alderman of Bristol, well learned in eating, knows by much experience—besides the delicious calipash and calipee, contains many different kinds of food ; nor can the learned reader be ignorant, that in human nature, though here collected under one general name, is such prodigious variety, that a cook will have sooner gone through all the several species of animal and vegetable food in the world, than an author will be able to exhaust so extensive a subject.

An objection may perhaps be apprehended from the more delicate, that this dish is too common and vulgar ; for what else is the subject of all the romances, novels, plays, and poems, with which the stalls abound ? Many exquisite viands might be rejected by the epicure if it was a sufficient cause for his contemning of them as common and vulgar, that something was to be found in the most paltry alleys under the same name. In reality, true nature is as difficult to be met with in authors, as the Bayonne ham, or Bologna sausage, is to be found in the shops.

But the whole, to continue the same metaphor, consists in the cookery of the author ; for, as Mr. Pope tells us—

> " True wit is nature to advantage drest ;
> What oft was thought, but ne'er so well exprest."

The same animal which hath the honour to have some part of his flesh eaten at the table of a duke, may perhaps be degraded in another part, and some of his limbs gibbeted, as it were, in the vilest stall in town. Where, then, lies the difference between the food of the nobleman and the porter, if both are at dinner on the same ox or calf, but in the seasoning, the dressing, the garnishing, and the setting forth ? Hence the one provokes and incites the most languid appetite, and the other turns and palls that which is the sharpest and keenest.

In like manner, the excellence of the mental entertainment consists less in the subject than in the author's skill in well dressing it up. How pleased, therefore, will the reader be to find that we have, in the following work, adhered closely to one of the highest principles of the best cook which the present age, or perhaps that of Heliogabalus, hath produced. This great man, as is well known to all lovers of polite eating, begins at first by setting plain things before his hungry guests, rising afterwards by degrees as their stomachs may be supposed to decrease, to the very quintessence of sauce and spices. In like manner, we shall represent human nature at first to the keen appetite of our reader, in that more plain and simple manner in which it is found in the country, and shall hereafter hash and ragoo it with all the high French and Italian seasoning of affectation and vice which courts and cities afford. By these means, we doubt not but our reader may be rendered desirous to read on for ever, as the great person just abovementioned is supposed to have made some persons eat.

Having premised thus much, we will now detain those who like our bill of fare no longer from their diet, and shall proceed directly to serve up the first course of our history for their entertainment.

Henry Fielding (1707–1754).

From " The History of Tom Jones.'

Beau Tibbs

Though naturally pensive, yet I am fond of gay company, and take every opportunity of thus dismissing the mind from duty. From this motive I am often found in the centre of a crowd ; and wherever pleasure is to be sold, am always a purchaser. In those places, without being remarked by any, I join in whatever goes forward ; work my passions into a similitude of frivolous earnestness, shout as they shout, and condemn as they happen to disapprove. A mind thus sunk for awhile below its natural standard, is qualified for stronger flights, as those first retire who would spring forward with greater vigour.

Attracted by the serenity of the evening, a friend and I lately went to gaze upon the company in one of the public walks near the city. Here we sauntered together for some time, either praising the beauty of such as were handsome, or the dresses of such as had nothing else to recommend them. We had gone thus deliberately forward for some time, when my friend, stopping on a sudden, caught me by the elbow, and led me out of the public walk. I could perceive by the quickness of his pace, and by his frequently looking behind, that he was attempting to avoid somebody who followed ; we now turned to the right, then to the left ; as we went forward, he still went faster, but in vain ; the person whom he attempted to escape, hunted us through every doubling, and gained upon us each moment; so that at last we fairly stood still, resolving to face what we could not avoid.

Our pursuer soon came up, and joined us with all the familiarity of an old acquaintance. "My dear Charles," cries he, shaking my friend's hand, "where have you been hiding this half a century? Positively I had fancied you were gone down to cultivate matrimony and your estate in the country." During the reply I had an opportunity of surveying the appearance of our new companion. His hat was pinched up with peculiar smartness; his looks were pale, thin, and sharp; round his neck he wore a broad black ribbon, and in his bosom a buckle studded with glass; his coat was trimmed with tarnished twist; he wore by his side a sword with a black hilt, and his stockings of silk, though newly washed, were grown yellow by long service. I was so much engaged with the peculiarity of his dress, that I attended only to the latter part of my friend's reply, in which he complimented Mr. Tibbs on the taste of his clothes, and the bloom in his countenance. "Psha, psha, Charles," cried the figure, "no more of that if you love me; you know I hate flattery, on my soul I do; and yet, to be sure, an intimacy with the great will improve one's appearance, and a course of venison will fatten; and yet, faith, I despise the great as much as you do; but there are a great many honest fellows among them; and we must not quarrel with one half because the other wants breeding. If they were all such as my Lord Mudler, one of the most good-natured creatures that ever squeezed a lemon, I should myself be among the number of their admirers. I was yesterday to dine at the Duchess of Piccadilly's. My lord was there. 'Ned,' says he to me, 'Ned,' says he, 'I'll hold gold to silver I can tell where you were poaching last night.' 'Poaching, my lord?' says I; 'faith, you have missed already; for I stayed at home, and let the girls poach for me. That's my way; I take a fine woman as some animals do their prey; stand still, and swoop, they fall into my mouth.'"

" Ah, Tibbs, thou art an happy fellow," cried my companion, with looks of infinite pity; " I hope your fortune is as much improved as your understanding in such company ? " " Improved," replied the other ; " you shall know—but let it go no further—a great secret— five hundred a year to begin with. My lord's word of honour for it. His lordship took me down in his own chariot yesterday, and we had a *tête-à-tête* dinner in the country ; where we talked of nothing else." " I fancy you forgot, sir," cried I ; " you told us but this moment of your dining yesterday in town." " Did I say so ? " replied he coolly. " To be sure, if I said so it was so. Dined in town : egad, now I do remember, I did dine in town ; but I dined in the country too ; for you must know, my boys, I eat two dinners. By the bye, I am grown as nice as the devil in my eating. I'll tell you a pleasant affair about that : We were a select party of us to dine at Lady Grogram's, an affected piece, but let it go no further ; a secret. ' Well,' says I, ' I'll hold a thousand guineas, and say done first, that——' But, dear Charles, you are an honest creature, lend me half a crown for a minute or two, or so, just till—— But, harkee, ask me for it the next time we meet, or it may be twenty to one but I forget to pay you."

When he left us, our conversation naturally turned upon so extraordinary a character. " His very dress," cries my friend, " is not less extraordinary than his conduct. If you meet him this day you find him in rags ; if the next, in embroidery. With those persons of distinction, of whom he talks so familiarly, he has scarce a coffee-house acquaintance. However, both for the interests of society, and perhaps for his own, Heaven has made him poor ; and while all the world perceives his

wants, he fancies them concealed from every eye. An
agreeable companion, because he understands flattery;
and all must be pleased with the first part of his conversation, though all are sure of its ending with a demand
on their purse. While his youth countenances the levity
of his conduct, he may thus earn a precarious subsistence; but when age comes on, the gravity of which is
incompatible with buffoonery, then will he find himself
forsaken by all; condemned, in the decline of life, to
hang upon some rich family whom he once despised,
there to undergo all the ingenuity of studied contempt,
to be employed only as a spy upon the servants, or a
bugbear to fright children into duty."

Oliver Goldsmith (1728–1774).

A Dissertation on the Art of Flying

Among the artists that had been allured into the
Happy Valley, to labour for the accommodation and
pleasure of its inhabitants, was a man eminent for his
knowledge of the mechanic powers, who had contrived
many engines both of use and recreation. By a wheel
which the stream turned, he forced the water into a
tower, whence it was distributed to all the apartments
of the palace. He erected a pavilion in the garden,
around which he kept the air always cool by artificial
showers. One of the groves, appropriated to the ladies,
was ventilated by fans, to which the rivulets that ran
through it gave a constant motion; and instruments
of soft music were played at proper distances, of which
some played by the impulse of the wind, and some by
the power of the stream.

This artist was sometimes visited by Rasselas, who
was pleased with every kind of knowledge, imagining

that the time would come when all his acquisitions should be of use to him in the open world. He came one day to amuse himself in his usual manner, and found the master busy in building a sailing chariot. He saw that the design was practicable upon a level surface, and with expressions of great esteem solicited its completion.

The workman was pleased to find himself so much regarded by the Prince, and resolved to gain yet higher honours.

"Sir," said he, "you have seen but a small part of what the mechanic sciences can perform. I have been long of opinion that, instead of the tardy conveyance of ships and chariots, man might use the swifter migration of wings; that the fields of air are open to knowledge, and that only ignorance and idleness need crawl upon the ground."

This hint rekindled the Prince's desire of passing the mountains. Having seen what the mechanist had already performed, he was willing to fancy that he could do more; yet resolved to inquire further before he suffered hope to afflict him by disappointment.

"I am afraid," said he to the artist, "that your imagination prevails over your skill, and that you now tell me rather what you wish than what you know. Every animal has his element assigned him; the birds have the air, and man and beasts the earth."

"So," replied the mechanist, "fishes have the water, in which yet beasts can swim by nature and man by art. He that can swim needs not despair to fly; to swim is to fly in a grosser fluid, and to fly is to swim in a subtler. We are only to proportion our power of resistance to the different density of matter through which we are to pass. You will be necessarily upborne by the air if you can renew any impulse upon it faster than the air can recede from the pressure."

" But the exercise of swimming," said the Prince, " is very laborious ; the strongest limbs are soon wearied. I am afraid the act of flying will be yet more violent ; and wings will be of no great use unless we can fly further than we can swim."

"The labour of rising from the ground," said the artist, " will be great, as we see it in the heavier domestic fowls ; but as we mount higher, the earth's attraction and the body's gravity will be gradually diminished, till we shall arrive at a region where the man shall float in the air without any tendency to fall ; no care will then be necessary but to move forward, which the gentlest impulse will effect. You, sir, whose curiosity is so extensive, will easily conceive with what pleasure a philosopher, furnished with wings and hovering in the sky, would see the earth and all its inhabitants rolling beneath him, and presenting to him successively, by its diurnal motion, all the countries within the same parallel. How must it amuse the pendent spectator to see the moving scene of land and ocean, cities and deserts ; to survey with equal security the marts of trade and the fields of battle ; mountains infested by barbarians, and fruitful regions gladdened by plenty and lulled by peace. How easily shall we then trace the Nile through all his passages, pass over to distant regions, and examine the face of Nature from one extremity of the earth to the other."

" All this," said the Prince, " is much to be desired, but I am afraid that no man will be able to breathe in these regions of speculation and tranquillity. I have been told that respiration is difficult upon lofty mountains ; yet from these precipices, though so high as to produce great tenuity of air, it is very easy to fall ; therefore I suspect that from any height where life can be supported, there may be danger of too quick descent."

" Nothing," replied the artist, " will ever be attempted

if all possible objections must be first overcome. If you will favour my project, I will try the first flight at my own hazard. I have considered the structure of all volant animals, and find the folding continuity of the bat's wings most easily accommodated to the human form. Upon this model I shall begin my task to-morrow; and in a year expect to tower into the air beyond the malice and pursuit of man. But I will work only on this condition : that the art shall not be divulged, and that you shall not require me to make wings for any but ourselves."

" Why," said Rasselas, " should you envy others so great an advantage ? All skill ought to be exerted for universal good ; every man has owed much to others, and ought to repay the kindness that he has received."

" If men were all virtuous," returned the artist, " I should with great alacrity teach them to fly. But what would be the security of the good if the bad could at pleasure invade them from the sky ? Against an army sailing through the clouds, neither walls, mountains, nor seas, could afford security. A flight of northern savages might hover in the wind, and light with irresistible violence upon the capital of a fruitful region. Even this valley, the retreat of princes, the abode of happiness, might be violated by the sudden descent of some of the naked nations that swarm on the coast of the southern sea ! "

The Prince promised secrecy, and waited for the performance, not wholly hopeless of success.

He visited the work from time to time, observed its progress, and remarked many ingenious contrivances to facilitate motion, and unite levity with strength. The artist was every day more certain that he should leave vultures and eagles behind him, and the contagion of his confidence seized upon the Prince. In a year the wings were finished ; and on a morning appointed the maker appeared, furnished for flight, on a little promontory : he waved his pinions a while to gather air, then leaped from his stand, and in an instant dropped into the lake. His wings, which were of no use in the air, sustained him in the water ; and the Prince drew him to land half dead with terror and vexation.

Samuel Johnson (1709–1784).

From " Rasselas."

A Passage from Roman History

The fertile province of Assyria, which stretched beyond the Tigris, as far as the mountains of Media, extended about four hundred miles from the ancient wall of Macepracta to the territory of Basra, where the united streams of the Euphrates and Tigris discharge themselves into the Persian Gulf. The whole country might have claimed the peculiar name of Mesopotamia, as the two rivers, which are never more distant than fifty, approach, between Bagdad and Babylon, within twenty-five miles of each other. A multitude of artificial canals, dug without much labour in a soft and yielding soil, connected the rivers and intersected the plain of Assyria. The uses of these artificial canals were various and important. They served to discharge the superfluous waters from one river into the other at the season of their respective inundations. Subdividing themselves into smaller and smaller branches, they refreshed the dry lands and supplied the deficiency of rain. They facilitated the intercourse of peace and commerce, and, as the dams could be speedily broke down, they armed the despair of the Assyrians with the means of opposing a sudden deluge to the progress of an invading army. To the soil and climate of Assyria nature had denied some of her choicest gifts—the vine, the olive, and the fig-tree ; but the food which supports the life of man, and particularly wheat and barley, were produced with inexhaustible fertility, and the husband-man, who committed his seed to the earth, was frequently rewarded with an increase of two or even of three hundred. The face of the country was interspersed with groves of innumerable palm-trees, and the diligent natives celebrated, either in verse or prose, the three hundred and sixty uses to which the trunk, the branches, the leaves, the juice, and the fruit were skilfully applied. Several manufactures, especially those of leather and linen, employed the industry of a numerous people, and afforded valuable materials for foreign trade, which appears, however, to have been conducted by the hands of strangers. Babylon had been converted into a royal park, but near the ruins of the ancient capital new cities had successively arisen, and the populousness of the country was displayed in the multitude of towns and villages, which were built of bricks dried in the sun and strongly cemented with bitumen, the natural and peculiar production of the Babylonian soil. While the successors of Cyrus reigned over Asia, the province of Assyria alone maintained, during a third part of the year, the luxurious plenty of the table and household of the Great King. Four considerable villages were assigned for the subsistence of his Indian dogs ; eight hundred stallions and sixteen thousand mares were constantly kept, at the expense of the country, for the royal stables ; and as the daily tribute which was paid to the satrap amounted to one English bushel of silver, we may compute the annual revenue of Assyria at more than twelve hundred thousand pounds sterling.

The fields of Assyria were devoted by Julian to the calamities of war ; and the philosopher retaliated on a guiltless people the acts of rapine and cruelty which had

been committed by their haughty master in the Roman
provinces. The trembling Assyrians summoned the
rivers to their assistance; and completed with their
own hands the ruin of their country. The roads were
rendered impracticable; a flood of waters was poured
into the camp; and, during several days, the troops of
Julian were obliged to contend with the most discourag-
ing hardships. But every obstacle was surmounted by
the perseverance of the legionaries, who were inured to
toil as well as to danger, and who felt themselves animated by the spirit of their leader. The damage was
gradually repaired; the waters were restored to their
proper channels; whole groves of palm-trees were cut
down and placed along the broken parts of the road;
and the army passed over the broad and deeper canals
on bridges of floating rafts, which were supported by
the help of bladders. Two cities of Assyria presumed
to resist the arms of a Roman emperor; and they both
paid the severe penalty of their rashness. At the distance of fifty miles from the royal residence of Ctesiphon,
Perisabor, or Anbar, held the second rank in the province: a city, large, populous, and well fortified, surrounded with a double wall, almost encompassed by a
branch of the Euphrates, and defended by the valour of
a numerous garrison. The exhortations of Hormisdas
were repulsed with contempt; and the ears of the Persian prince were wounded by a just reproach, that,
unmindful of his royal birth, he conducted an army of
strangers against his king and country. The Assyrians
maintained their loyalty by a skilful as well as vigorous
defence, till the lucky stroke of a battering-ram having
opened a large breach by shattering one of the angles
of the wall, they hastily retired into the fortifications of
the interior citadel. The soldiers of Julian rushed impetuously into the town, and, after the full gratification
of every military appetite, Perisabor was reduced to

ashes ; and the engines which assaulted the citadel were planted on the ruins of the smoking houses. The contest was continued by an incessant and mutual discharge of missile weapons ; and the superiority which the Romans might derive from the mechanical powers of their balistæ and catapultæ was counterbalanced by the advantage of the ground on the side of the besieged. But as soon as an *Helepolis* had been constructed, which could engage on equal terms with the loftiest ramparts, the tremendous aspect of a moving turret, that would leave no hope of resistance or of mercy, terrified the defenders of the citadel into an humble submission ; and the place was surrendered only two days after Julian first appeared under the walls of Perisabor. Two thousand five hundred persons of both sexes, the feeble remnant of a flourishing people, were permitted to retire : the plentiful magazines of corn, of arms, and of splendid furniture, were partly distributed among the troops and partly reserved for the public service ; the useless stores were destroyed by fire or thrown into the stream of the Euphrates ; and the fate of Amida was revenged by the total ruin of Perisabor.

The city, or rather fortress, of Maogamalcha, which was defended by sixteen large towers, a deep ditch, and two strong and solid walls of brick and bitumen, appears to have been constructed at the distance of eleven miles, as the safeguard of the capital of Persia. The emperor, apprehensive of leaving such an important fortress in his rear, immediately formed the siege of Maogamalcha ; and the Roman army was distributed for that purpose into three divisions. Victor, at the head of the cavalry and of a detachment of heavy-armed foot, was ordered to clear the country as far as the banks of the Tigris and the suburbs of Ctesiphon. The conduct of the attack was assumed by Julian himself, who seemed to place his whole dependence in the military engines which he erected against the walls ; while he secretly contrived a more efficacious method of introducing his troops into the heart of the city. Under the direction of Nevitta and Dagalaiphus, the trenches were opened at a considerable distance, and gradually prolonged as far as the edge of the ditch. The ditch was speedily filled with earth ; and, by the incessant labour of the troops, a mine was carried under the foundations of the walls, and sustained at sufficient intervals by props of timber. Three chosen cohorts, advancing in a single file, silently explored the dark and dangerous passage ; till their intrepid leader whispered back the intelligence that he was ready to issue from his confinement into the streets of the hostile city. Julian checked their ardour, that he might ensure their success ; and immediately diverted the attention of the garrison by the tumult and clamour of a general assault. The Persians, who from their walls contemptuously beheld the progress of an impotent attack, celebrated with songs of triumph the glory of Sapor ; and ventured to assure the emperor that he might ascend the starry mansion of Ormusd before he could hope to take the impregnable city of Maogamalcha. The city was already taken. History has recorded the name of a private soldier, the first who ascended from the mine into a deserted tower. The passage was widened by his companions, who pressed forwards with impatient valour. Fifteen hundred enemies were already in the midst of the city. The astonished garrison abandoned the walls, and their only hope of safety ; the gates were instantly burst open ; and the revenge of the soldier, unless it were suspended by lust or avarice, was satiated by an undistinguishing massacre. The governor, who had yielded on a promise of mercy, was burnt alive, a few days afterwards, on a charge of having uttered some disrespectful words against the honour of Prince Hormisdas. The fortifications were

razed to the ground ; and not a vestige was left that
the city of Maogamalcha had ever existed. The neighbourhood of the capital of Persia was adorned with three
stately palaces, laboriously enriched with every production that could gratify the luxury and pride of an
Eastern monarch. The pleasant situation of the gardens along the banks of the Tigris was improved, according to the Persian taste, by the symmetry of flowers,
fountains, and shady walks : and spacious parks were
enclosed for the reception of the bears, lions, and wild
boars, which were maintained at a considerable expense
for the pleasure of the royal chase. The park-walls were
broken down, the savage game was abandoned to the
darts of the soldiers, and the palaces of Sapor were
reduced to ashes, by the command of the Roman emperor. Julian, on this occasion, showed himself ignorant
or careless of the laws of civility, which the prudence
and refinement of polished ages have established between
hostile princes. Yet these wanton ravages need not
excite in our breasts any vehement emotions of pity or
resentment. A simple, naked statue, finished by the
hand of a Grecian artist, is of more genuine value than
all these rude and costly monuments of barbaric labour ;
and, if we are more deeply affected by the ruin of a
palace than by the conflagration of a cottage, our humanity must have formed a very erroneous estimate of the
miseries of human life.

Julian was an object of terror and hatred to the Persians ; and the painters of that nation represented the
invader of their country under the emblem of a furious
lion, who vomited from his mouth a consuming fire. To
his friends and soldiers the philosophic hero appeared in
a more amiable light ; and his virtues were never more
conspicuously displayed than in the last and most active
period of his life. When the Romans marched through
the flat and flooded country, their sovereign, on foot,

at the head of his legions, shared their fatigues and animated their diligence. In every useful labour the hand of Julian was prompt and strenuous; and the Imperial purple was wet and dirty, as the coarse garment of the meanest soldier. The two sieges allowed him some remarkable opportunities of signalizing his personal valour, which, in the improved state of the military art, can seldom be exerted by a prudent general. The emperor stood before the citadel of Perisabor, insensible of his extreme danger, and encouraged his troops to burst open the gates of iron, till he was almost overwhelmed under a cloud of missile weapons and huge stones that were directed against his person. As he examined the exterior fortifications of Maogamalcha, two Persians, devoting themselves for their country, suddenly rushed upon him with drawn scimitars: the emperor dexterously received their blows on his uplifted shield; and, with a steady and well-aimed thrust, laid one of his adversaries dead at his feet. The esteem of a prince who possesses the virtues which he approves is the noblest recompense of a deserving subject; and the authority which Julian derived from his personal merit enabled him to revive and enforce the rigour of ancient discipline. He punished with death, or ignominy, the misbehaviour of three troops of horse, who, in a skirmish with the Surenas, had lost their honour and one of their standards: and he distinguished with *obsidional* crowns the valour of the foremost soldiers who had ascended into the city of Maogamalcha. After the siege of Perisabor the firmness of the emperor was exercised by the insolent avarice of the army, who loudly complained that their services were rewarded by a trifling donative of one hundred pieces of silver. His just indignation was expressed in the grave and manly language of a Roman. " Riches are the object of your desires; those riches are in the hands of the Persians; and the spoils of this fruitful country are proposed as the prize of your valour and discipline. Believe me," added Julian, " the Roman republic, which formerly possessed such immense treasures, is now reduced to want and wretchedness ; since our princes have been persuaded, by weak and interested ministers, to purchase with gold the tranquillity of the barbarians. The revenue is exhausted ; the cities are ruined ; the provinces are dispeopled. For myself, the only inheritance that I have received from my royal ancestors is a soul incapable of fear ; and as long as I am convinced that every real advantage is seated in the mind, I shall not blush to acknowledge an honourable poverty, which in the days of ancient virtue was considered as the glory of Fabricius. That glory, and that virtue, may be your own, if you will listen to the voice of Heaven and of your leader. But if you will rashly persist, if you are determined to renew the shameful and mischievous examples of old seditions, proceed. As it becomes an emperor who has filled the first rank among men, I am prepared to die standing, and to despise a precarious life which every hour may depend on an accidental fever. If I have been found unworthy of the command, there are now among you (I speak it with pride and pleasure), there are many chiefs whose merit and experience are equal to the conduct of the most important war. Such has been the temper of my reign, that I can retire, without regret and without apprehension, to the obscurity of a private station." The modest resolution of Julian was answered by the unanimous applause and cheerful obedience of the Romans, who declared their confidence of victory while they fought under the banners of their heroic prince. Their courage was kindled by his frequent and familiar asseverations (for such wishes were the oaths of Julian), " So may I reduce the Persians under the yoke ! " " Thus may I restore the strength and splendour of the republic ! "

The love of fame was the ardent passion of his soul : but it was not before he trampled on the ruins of Maogamalcha that he allowed himself to say, " We have now provided some materials for the sophist of Antioch."

The successful valour of Julian had triumphed over all the obstacles that opposed his march to the gates of Ctesiphon. But the reduction, or even the siege, of the capital of Persia was still at a distance : nor can the military conduct of the emperor be clearly apprehended without a knowledge of the country which was the theatre of his bold and skilful operations. Twenty miles to the south of Bagdad, and on the eastern bank of the Tigris, the curiosity of travellers has observed some ruins of the palaces of Ctesiphon, which in the time of Julian was a great and populous city. The name and glory of the adjacent Seleucia were for ever extinguished ; and the only remaining quarter of that Greek colony had resumed, with the Assyrian language and manners, the primitive appellation of Coche. Coche was situate on the western side of the Tigris ; but it was naturally considered as a suburb of Ctesiphon, with which we may suppose it to have been connected by a permanent bridge of boats. The united parts contributed to form the common epithet of Al Modain, THE CITIES, which the Orientals have bestowed on the winter residence of the Sassanides ; and the whole circumference of the Persian capital was strongly fortified by the waters of the river, by lofty walls, and by impracticable morasses. Near the ruins of Seleucia the camp of Julian was fixed, and secured by a ditch and rampart against the sallies of the numerous and enterprising garrison of Coche. In this fruitful and pleasant country the Romans were plentifully supplied with water and forage : and several forts, which might have embarrassed the motions of the army, submitted, after some resistance, to the efforts of their valour. The fleet passed from the Euphrates into an

artificial deviation of that river, which pours a copious
and navigable stream into the Tigris at a small distance
below the great city. If they had followed this royal
canal, which bore the name of Nahar-Malcha, the inter-
mediate situation of Coche would have separated the
fleet and army of Julian ; and the rash attempt of steering against the current of the Tigris, and forcing their
way through the midst of a hostile capital, must have
been attended with the total destruction of the Roman
navy. The prudence of the emperor foresaw the danger, and provided the remedy. As he had minutely
studied the operations of Trajan in the same country,
he soon recollected that his warlike predecessor had dug
a new and navigable canal, which, leaving Coche on the
right hand, conveyed the waters of the Nahar-Malcha
into the river Tigris at some distance *above* the cities.
From the information of the peasants Julian ascertained
the vestiges of this ancient work, which were almost
obliterated by design or accident. By the indefatigable
labour of the soldiers a broad and deep channel was
speedily prepared for the reception of the Euphrates.
A strong dyke was constructed to interrupt the ordinary
current of the Nahar-Malcha : a flood of waters rushed
impetuously into their new bed ; and the Roman fleet,
steering their triumphant course into the Tigris, derided
the vain and ineffectual barriers which the Persians of
Ctesiphon had erected to oppose their passage.

As it became necessary to transport the Roman army
over the Tigris, another labour presented itself, of less
toil, but of more danger, than the preceding expedition.
The stream was broad and rapid, the ascent steep and
difficult ; and the entrenchments which had been formed
on the ridge of the opposite bank were lined with a
numerous army of heavy cuirassiers, dexterous archers,
and huge elephants ; who (according to the extravagant
hyperbole of Libanius) could trample with the same ease

a field of corn or a legion of Romans. In the presence
of such an enemy the construction of a bridge was impracticable ; and the intrepid prince, who instantly
seized the only possible expedient, concealed his design,
till the moment of execution, from the knowledge of the
barbarians, of his own troops, and even of his generals
themselves. Under the specious pretence of examining
the state of the magazines, fourscore vessels were gradually unladen ; and a select detachment, apparently
destined for some secret expedition, was ordered to stand
to their arms on the first signal. Julian disguised the
silent anxiety of his own mind with smiles of confidence
and joy ; and amused the hostile nations with the
spectacle of military games, which he insultingly celebrated under the walls of Coche. The day was conse-
crated to pleasure ; but, as soon as the hour of supper
was past, the emperor summoned the generals to his
tent, and acquainted them that he had fixed that night
for the passage of the Tigris. They stood in silent and
respectful astonishment ; but when the venerable Sallust
assumed the privilege of his age and experience, the rest
of the chiefs supported with freedom the weight of his
prudent remonstrances. Julian contented himself with
observing that conquest and safety depended on the
attempt ; that, instead of diminishing, the number of
their enemies would be increased by successive reinforcements ; and that a longer delay would neither contract
the breadth of the stream nor level the height of the
bank. The signal was instantly given, and obeyed : the
most impatient of the legionaries leaped into five vessels
that lay nearest to the bank ; and, as they plied their
oars with intrepid diligence, they were lost after a few
moments in the darkness of the night. A flame arose
on the opposite side ; and Julian, who too clearly understood that his foremost vessels in attempting to land
had been fired by the enemy, dexterously converted their

extreme danger into a presage of victory. " Our fellow-soldiers," he eagerly exclaimed, " are already masters of the bank : see—they make the appointed signal ; let us hasten to emulate and assist their courage." The united and rapid motion of a great fleet broke the violence of the current, and they reached the eastern shore of the Tigris with sufficient speed to extinguish the flames and rescue their adventurous companions. The difficulties of a steep and lofty ascent were increased by the weight of armour and the darkness of the night. A shower of stones, darts, and fire was incessantly discharged on the heads of the assailants ; who, after an arduous struggle, climbed the bank and stood victorious upon the rampart. As soon as they possessed a more equal field, Julian, who with his light infantry had led the attack, darted through the ranks a skilful and experienced eye : his bravest soldiers, according to the precepts of Homer, were distributed in the front and rear ; and all the trumpets of the Imperial army sounded to battle. The Romans, after sending up a military shout, advanced in measured steps to the animating notes of martial music ; launched their formidable javelins, and rushed forwards with drawn swords to deprive the barbarians, by a closer onset, of the advantage of their missile weapons. The whole engagement lasted above twelve hours ; till the gradual retreat of the Persians was changed into a disorderly flight, of which the shameful example was given by the principal leaders and the Surenas himself. They were pursued to the gates of Ctesiphon ; and the conquerors might have entered the dismayed city, if their general, Victor, who was dangerously wounded with an arrow, had not conjured them to desist from a rash attempt, which must be fatal if it were not successful. On *their* side the Romans acknowledged the loss of only seventy-five men ; while they affirmed that the barbarians had left on the field of battle two thousand five hundred, or even six thousand, of their bravest soldiers. The spoil was such as might be expected from the riches and luxury of an Oriental camp; large quantities of silver and gold, splendid arms and trappings, and beds and tables of massive silver. The victorious emperor distributed, as the rewards of valour, some honourable gifts, civic, and mural, and naval crowns; which he, and perhaps he alone, esteemed more precious than the wealth of Asia. A solemn sacrifice was offered to the god of war, but the appearances of the victims threatened the most inauspicious events; and Julian soon discovered, by less ambiguous signs, that he had now reached the term of his prosperity.

Edward Gibbon (1737–1794).

From " The Decline and Fall of the Roman Empire."

The End of a Famous Open Letter

I am constantly of opinion, that your states, in three orders, on the footing on which they stood in 1614, were capable of being brought into a proper and harmonious combination with royal authority. This constitution by estates, was the natural and only just representation of France. It grew out of the habitual conditions, relations, and reciprocal claims of men. It grew out of the circumstances of the country, and out of the state of property. The wretched scheme of your present masters is not to fit the constitution to the people, but wholly to destroy conditions, to dissolve relations, to change the state of the nation, and to subvert property, in order to fit their country to their theory of a constitution.

Until you make out practically that great work, a combination of opposing forces, " a work of labour long,

and endless praise," the utmost caution ought to have
been used in the reduction of the royal power, which
alone was capable of holding together the comparatively
heterogeneous mass of your states. But, at this day,
all these considerations are unseasonable. To what end
should we discuss the limitations of royal power ? Your
king is in prison. Why speculate on the measure and
standard of liberty ? I doubt much, very much indeed,
whether France is at all ripe for liberty on any standard.
Men are qualified for civil liberty in exact proportion to
their disposition to put moral chains upon their own
appetites ; in proportion as their love to justice is above
their rapacity ; in proportion as their soundness and
sobriety of understanding is above their vanity and
presumption ; in proportion as they are more disposed
to listen to the counsels of the wise and good, in prefer-
ence to the flattery of knaves. Society cannot exist
unless a controlling power upon will and appetite be
placed somewhere, and the less of it there is within,
the more there must be without. It is ordained in the
eternal constitution of things, that men of intemperate
minds cannot be free. Their passions forge their fetters.

This sentence the prevalent part of your countrymen
execute on themselves. They possessed not long since,
what was next to freedom, a mild paternal monarchy.
They despised it for its weakness. They were offered
a well-poised, free constitution. It did not suit their
taste nor their temper. They carved for themselves ;
they flew out, murdered, robbed, and rebelled. They
have succeeded, and put over their country an insolent
tyranny made up of cruel and inexorable masters, and
that too of a description hitherto not known in the
world. The powers and policies by which they have
succeeded are not those of great statesmen, or great
military commanders, but the practices of incendiaries,
assassins, housebreakers, robbers, spreaders of false news,

forgers of false orders from authority, and other delin-
quencies, of which ordinary justice takes cognizance.
Accordingly the spirit of their rule is exactly corre-
spondent to the means by which they obtained it. They
act more in the manner of thieves who have got possession of a house, than of conquerors who have subdued a
nation.

Opposed to these in appearance, but in appearance
only, is another band, who call themselves the *moderate*.
These, if I conceive rightly of their conduct, are a set
of men who approve heartily of the whole new constitution, but wish to lay heavily on the most atrocious of
those crimes, by which this fine constitution of theirs
has been obtained. They are a sort of people who
affect to proceed as if they thought that men may
deceive without fraud, rob without injustice, and over-
turn everything without violence. They are men who
would usurp the government of their country with
decency and moderation. In fact, they are nothing
more or better, than men engaged in desperate designs,
with feeble minds. They are not honest; they are only
ineffectual and unsystematic in their iniquity. They
are persons who want not the dispositions, but the
energy and vigour, that is necessary for great evil
machinations. They find that in such designs they fall
at best into a secondary rank, and others take the place
and lead in usurpation, which they are not qualified
to obtain or to hold. They envy to their companions
the natural fruit of their crimes; they join to run them
down with the hue and cry of mankind, which pursues
their common offences; and then hope to mount into
their places on the credit of the sobriety with which
they show themselves disposed to carry on what may
seem most plausible in the mischievous projects they
pursue in common. But these men are naturally despised by those who have heads to know, and hearts

that are able to go through, the necessary demands of bold wicked enterprises. They are naturally classed below the latter description, and will only be used by them as inferior instruments. They will be only the Fairfaxes of your Cromwells. If they mean honestly, why do they not strengthen the arms of honest men, to support their ancient, legal, wise, and free government, given to them in the spring of 1788, against the inventions of craft, and the theories of ignorance and folly ? If they do not, they must continue the scorn of both parties ; sometimes the tool, sometimes the encumbrance, of that, whose views they approve, whose conduct they decry. These people are only made to be the sport of tyrants. They never can obtain or communicate freedom.

You ask me too, whether we have a committee of research. No, Sir,—God forbid ! It is the necessary instrument of tyranny and usurpation; and therefore I do not wonder that it has had an early establishment under your present lords. We do not want it.

Excuse my length. I have been somewhat occupied since I was honoured with your letter ; and I should not have been able to answer it at all, but for the holidays, which have given me means of enjoying the leisure of the country. I am called to duties which I am neither able nor willing to evade. I must soon return to my old conflict with the corruptions and oppressions which have prevailed in our eastern dominions. I must turn myself wholly from those of France.

In England we *cannot* work so hard as Frenchmen. Frequent relaxation is necessary to us. You are naturally more intense in your application. I did not know this part of your national character, until I went into France in 1773. At present, this your disposition to labour is rather increased than lessened. In your Assembly you do not allow yourselves a recess even on

Sundays. We have two days in the week, besides the festivals ; and besides five or six months of the summer and autumn. This continued, unremitted effort of the members of your Assembly, I take to be one among the causes of the mischief they have done. They who always labour can have no true judgment. You never give yourselves time to cool. You can never survey, from its proper point of sight, the work you have finished, before you decree its final execution. You can never plan the future by the past. You never go into the country, soberly and dispassionately to observe the effect of your measures on their objects. You cannot feel distinctly how far the people are rendered better and improved, or more miserable and depraved, by what you have done. You cannot see with your own eyes the sufferings and afflictions you cause. You know them but at a distance, on the statements of those who always flatter the reigning power, and who, amidst their representations of the grievances, inflame your minds against those who are oppressed. These are amongst the effects of unremitted labour, when men exhaust their attention, burn out their candles, and are left in the dark.—*Malo meorum negligentiam, quam istorum obscuram diligentiam.*

I have the honour, &c.

(Signed) EDMUND BURKE.

Beaconsfield, January 19th, 1791.

From " A Letter to a Member of the National Assembly."

Burns and His Poetry

The following trifles are not the production of the Poet, who, with all the advantages of learned art, and, perhaps, amid the elegancies and idleness of upper life, looks down for a rural theme, with an eye to Theocritus or Virgil. To the Author of this, these, and other celebrated names, their countrymen are, at least in their original language, " a fountain shut up, and a book sealed." Unacquainted with the necessary requisites for commencing poet by rule, he sings the sentiments and manners he felt and saw in himself and his rustic compeers around him, in his and their native language. Though a rhymer from his earliest years, at least from the earliest impulse of the softer passions, it was not till very lately that the applause, perhaps the partiality of friendship, awakened his vanity so far as to make him think anything of his worth showing : and none of the following works were composed with a view to the press. To amuse himself with the little creations of his own fancy, amid the toil and fatigue of a laborious life ; to transcribe the various feelings—the loves, the griefs, the hopes, the fears—in his own breast ; to find some kind of counterpoise to the struggles of a world, always an alien scene, a task uncouth to the poetical mind—these were his motives for courting the Muses, and in these he found Poetry to be its own reward.

Now that he appears in the public character of an Author, he does it with fear and trembling. So dear is fame to the rhyming tribe, that even he, an obscure, nameless Bard, shrinks aghast at the thought of being branded as—an impertinent blockhead, obtruding his nonsense on the world ; and, because he can make shift to jingle a few doggerel Scottish rhymes together, looking upon himself as a poet, of no small consequence, forsooth !

It is an observation of that celebrated poet, Shenstone, whose divine Elegies do honour to our language, our nation, and our species, that " Humility has depressed many a genius to a hermit, but never raised one to fame ! " If any critic catches at the word Genius, the author tells him, once for all, that he certainly looks upon himself as possessed of some poetic abilities, otherwise his publishing, in the manner he has done, would be a manœuvre below the worst character which, he hopes, his worst enemy will ever give him. But to the genius of a Ramsay, or the glorious dawnings of the poor unfortunate Fergusson, he, with equal unaffected sincerity, declares that, even in his highest pulse of vanity, he has not the most distant pretensions. These two justly admired Scottish poets he has often had in his eye in the following pieces ; but rather with a view to kindle at their flame than for servile imitation.

To his Subscribers the Author returns his most sincere thanks. Not the mercenary bow over a counter, but the heart-throbbing gratitude of the Bard, conscious how much he owes to benevolence and friendship for gratifying him, if he deserves it, in that dearest wish of every poetic bosom—to be distinguished. He begs his readers, particularly the learned and the polite, who may honour him with a perusal, that they will make every allowance for education and circumstances of life ; but if, after a fair, candid, and impartial criticism, he shall stand convicted of dulness and nonsense, let him be done by as he would in that case do by others —let him be condemned, without mercy, to contempt and oblivion.

Robert Burns (1759–1796).

The Preface to the First, or Kilmarnock,
Edition of his Poems, July, 1786.

My First Play

At the north end of Cross-court there yet stands a portal, of some architectural pretensions, though re-

duced to humble use, serving at present for an entrance
to a printing-office. This old door-way, if you are
young, reader, you may not know was the identical
pit entrance to old Drury—Garrick's Drury—all of it
that is left. I never pass it without shaking some
forty years from off my shoulders, recurring to the
evening when I passed through it to see *my first play.*
The afternoon had been wet, and the condition of our
going (the elder folks and myself) was, that the rain
should cease. With what a beating heart did I watch
from the window the puddles, from the stillness of which
I was taught to prognosticate the desired cessation!
I seem to remember the last spurt, and the glee with
which I ran to announce it.

We went with orders, which my godfather F. had
sent us. He kept the oil shop (now Davies's) at the
corner of Featherstone-buildings, in Holborn. F. was
a tall grave person, lofty in speech, and had pretensions
above his rank. He associated in those days with
John Palmer, the comedian, whose gait and bearing he
seemed to copy; if John (which is quite as likely) did
not rather borrow somewhat of his manner from my godfather. He was also known to, and visited by, Sheridan.
It was to his house in Holborn that young Brinsley
brought his first wife on her elopement with him from a
boarding-school at Bath—the beautiful Maria Linley. My
parents were present (over a quadrille table) when he arrived in the evening with his harmonious charge. From
either of these connexions it may be inferred that my
godfather could command an order for the then Drury-
lane theatre at pleasure—and, indeed, a pretty liberal
issue of those cheap billets, in Brinsley's easy auto-
graph, I have heard him say was the sole remunera-
tion which he had received for many years' nightly
illumination of the orchestra and various avenues of
that theatre—and he was content it should be so. The

honour of Sheridan's familiarity—or supposed familiarity
—was better to my godfather than money.

F. was the most gentlemanly of oilmen ; grandilo-
quent, yet courteous. His delivery of the commonest
matters of fact was Ciceronian. He had two Latin
words almost constantly in his mouth (how odd sounds
Latin from an oilman's lips !), which my better knowledge since has enabled me to correct. In strict pronunciation they should have been sounded *vice versâ*
—but in those young years they impressed me with more
awe than they would now do, read aright from Seneca
or Varro—in his own peculiar pronunciation, mono-
syllabically elaborated, or Anglicized, into something
like *verse verse.* By an imposing manner, and the help
of these distorted syllables, he climbed (but that
was little) to the highest parochial honours which St.
Andrew's has to bestow.

He is dead—and thus much I thought due to his
memory, both for my first orders (little wondrous
talismans !—slight keys, and insignificant to outward
sight, but opening to me more than Arabian paradises !)
and moreover that by his testamentary beneficence I
came into possession of the only landed property which
I could ever call my own—situate near the road-way
village of pleasant Puckeridge, in Hertfordshire. When
I journeyed down to take possession, and planted foot
on my own ground, the stately habits of the donor
descended upon me, and I strode (shall I confess the
vanity ?) with larger paces over my allotment of three
quarters of an acre, with its commodious mansion in
the midst, with the feeling of an English freeholder that
all betwixt sky and centre was my own. The estate
has passed into more prudent hands, and nothing but
an agrarian can restore it.

In those days were pit orders. Beshrew the uncom-
fortable manager who abolished them !—with one of

these we went. I remember the waiting at the door
—not that which is left—but between that and an
inner door in shelter—O when shall I be such an ex-
pectant again !—with the cry of nonpareils, an indispensable play-house accompaniment in those days. As
near as I can recollect, the fashionable pronunciation of
the theatrical fruiteresses then was " Chase some oranges,
chase some numparels, chase a bill of the play ; "—
chase *pro* chuse. But when we got in, and I beheld
the green curtain that veiled a heaven to my imagination, which was soon to be disclosed—the breathless
anticipations I endured ! I had seen something like it
in the plate prefixed to Troilus and Cressida, in Rowe's
Shakespeare—the tent scene with Diomede—and a
sight of that plate can always bring back in a measure
the feeling of that evening.—The boxes at that time, full
of well-dressed women of quality, projected over the
pit : and the pilasters reaching down were adorned
with a glistering substance (I know not what) under
glass (as it seemed), resembling—a homely fancy—
but I judged it to be sugar-candy—yet, to my raised
imagination, divested of its homelier qualities, it appeared a glorified candy !—The orchestra lights at
length arose, those " fair Auroras ! " Once the bell
sounded. It was to ring out yet once again—and,
incapable of the anticipation, I reposed my shut eyes
in a sort of resignation upon the maternal lap. It
rang the second time. The curtain drew up—I was
not past six years old and the play was Artaxerxes !

I had dabbled a little in the Universal History—the
ancient part of it—and here was the court of Persia.—
It was being admitted to a sight of the past. I took
no proper interest in the action going on, for I understood not its import—but I heard the word Darius, and
I was in the midst of Daniel. All feeling was absorbed
in vision. Gorgeous vests, gardens, palaces, princesses,

passed before me. I knew not players. I was in
Persepolis for the time, and the burning idol of their
devotion almost converted me into a worshipper. I
was awe-struck, and believed those significations to be
something more than elemental fires. It was all en-
chantment and a dream. No such pleasure has since
visited me but in dreams.—Harlequin's invasion followed ; where, I remember, the transformation of the
magistrates into reverend beldams seemed to me a
piece of grave historic justice, and the tailor carrying
his own head to be as sober a verity as the legend of
St. Denys.

The next play to which I was taken was the Lady
of the Manor, of which, with the exception of some
scenery, very faint traces are left in my memory. It
was followed by a pantomime, called Lun's Ghost—
a satiric touch, I apprehend, upon Rich, not long since
dead—but to my apprehension (too sincere for satire),
Lun was as remote a piece of antiquity as Lud—the
father of a line of Harlequins—transmitting his dagger
of lath (the wooden sceptre) through countless ages. I
saw the primeval Motley come from his silent tomb in
a ghastly vest of white patch-work, like the apparition
of a dead rainbow. So Harlequins (thought I) look
when they are dead.

My third play followed in quick succession. It was
the Way of the World. I think I must have sat at it
as grave as a judge ; for, I remember, the hysteric
affectations of good Lady Wishfort affected me like some
solemn tragic passion. Robinson Crusoe followed ; in
which Crusoe, man Friday, and the parrot, were as
good and authentic as in the story.—The clownery and
pantaloonery of these pantomimes have clean passed
out of my head. I believe, I no more laughed at them,
than at the same age I should have been disposed to
laugh at the grotesque Gothic heads (seeming to me

then replete with devout meaning) that gape, and grin, in stone around the inside of the old Round Church (my church) of the Templars.

I saw these plays in the season 1781-2, when I was from six to seven years old. After the intervention of six or seven other years (for at school all play-going was inhibited) I again entered the doors of a theatre. That old Artaxerxes evening had never done ringing in my fancy. I expected the same feelings to come again with the same occasion. But we differ from ourselves less at sixty and sixteen, than the latter does from six. In that interval what had I not lost! At the first period I knew nothing, understood nothing, discriminated nothing. I felt all, loved all, wondered all—

> Was nourished, I could not tell how—

I had left the temple a devotee, and was returned a rationalist. The same things were there materially; but the emblem, the reference, was gone!—The green curtain was no longer a veil, drawn between two worlds, the unfolding of which was to bring back past ages to present a "royal ghost,"—but a certain quantity of green baize, which was to separate the audience for a given time from certain of their fellow-men who were to come forward and pretend those parts. The lights—the orchestra lights—came up a clumsy machinery. The first ring, and the second ring, was now but a trick of the prompter's bell—which had been, like the note of the cuckoo, a phantom of a voice, no hand seen or guessed at which ministered to its warning. The actors were men and women painted. I thought the fault was in them; but it was in myself, and the alteration which those many centuries,—of six short twelvemonths—had wrought in me.—Perhaps it was fortunate for me that the play of the evening was but an indifferent comedy, as it gave me time to crop some unreasonable

expectations, which might have interfered with the
genuine emotions with which I was soon after enabled
to enter upon the first appearance to me of Mrs. Siddons
in Isabella. Comparison and retrospection soon yielded
to the present attraction of the scene ; and the theatre
became to me, upon a new stock, the most delightful
of recreations.

Charles Lamb (1775–1834).

From " Essays of Elia."

The Chase and After

The drivers thorough the wood went,
  For to raise the deer ;
Bowmen bickered upon the bent,
  With their broad arrows clear.

The wylde thorough the woods went,
  On every side shear ;
Grehounds thorough the groves glent,
  For to kill thir deer.

  Ballad of Chevy Chase, Old Edit.

The appointed morning came in cold and raw, after the
manner of the Scottish March weather. Dogs yelped,
yawned, and shivered, and the huntsmen, though hardy
and cheerful in expectation of the day's sport, twitched
their mawds, or Lowland plaids, close to their throats,
and looked with some dismay at the mists which floated
about the horizon, now threatening to sink down on
the peaks and ridges of prominent mountains, and
now to shift their position under the influence of some
of the uncertain gales, which rose and fell alternately,
as they swept along the valley.

Nevertheless the appearance of the whole formed,
as is usual in almost all departments of the chase, a
gay and a jovial spectacle. A brief truce seemed to

have taken place between the nations, and the Scottish people appeared for the time rather as exhibiting the sports of their mountains in a friendly manner to the accomplished knights and bonny archers of Old England, than as performing a feudal service, neither easy nor dignified in itself, at the instigation of usurping neighbours. The figures of the cavaliers, now half seen, now exhibited fully, and at the height of strenuous exertion, according to the character of the dangerous and broken ground, particularly attracted the attention of the pedestrians, who, leading the dogs or beating the thickets, dislodged such objects of chase as they found in the dingles, and kept their eyes fixed upon their companions, rendered more remarkable from being mounted, and the speed at which they urged their horses ; the disregard of all accidents being as perfect as Melton Mowbray itself or any other noted field of hunters of the present day, can exhibit.

The principles on which modern and ancient hunting were conducted, are, however, as different as possible. A fox, or even a hare is, in our own day, considered as a sufficient apology for a day's exercise to forty or fifty dogs, and nearly as many men and horses ; but the ancient chase, even though not terminating, as it often did, in battle, carried with it objects more important, and an interest immeasurably more stirring. If indeed one species of exercise can be pointed out as more universally exhilarating and engrossing than others, it is certainly that of the chase. The poor over-laboured drudge, who has served out his day of life, and wearied all his energies in the service of his fellow-mortals—he who has been for many years the slave of agriculture, or (still worse) of manufactures —engaged in raising a single peck of corn from year to year, or in the monotonous labours of the desk— can hardly remain dead to the general happiness when

the chase sweeps past him with hound and horn, and
for a moment feels all the exultation of the proudest
cavalier who partakes the amusement. Let any one who
has witnessed the sight, recall to his imagination the
vigour and lively interest which he has seen inspired
into a village, including the oldest and feeblest of its
inhabitants. In the words of Wordsworth, it is, on
such occasions,

" Up, Timothy, up with your staff and away,
Not a soul will remain in the village to-day,
The hare has just started from Hamilton's grounds,
And Skiddaw is glad with the cry of the hounds."

But compare these inspiring sounds to the burst of a
whole feudal population enjoying the sport, whose lives,
instead of being spent in the monotonous toil of modern
avocations, have been agitated by the hazards of war,
and of the chase, its near resemblance, and you must
necessarily suppose that the excitation is extended, like
a fire which catches to dry heath. To use the common
expression, borrowed from another amusement, all is
fish that comes in the net on such occasions. An
ancient hunting-match (the nature of the carnage excepted) was almost equal to a modern battle, when the
strife took place on the surface of a varied and unequal
country. A whole district poured forth its inhabitants,
who formed a ring of great extent, called technically a
tinchel, and, advancing and narrowing their circle
by degrees, drove before them the alarmed animals of
every kind ; all and each of which, as they burst from
the thicket or the moorland, were objects of the bow,
the javelin, or whatever missile weapons the hunters
possessed ; while others were run down and worried by
large greyhounds, or more frequently brought to bay,
when the more important persons present claimed for
themselves the pleasure of putting them to death with
their chivalrous hands, incurring individually such

danger as is inferred from a mortal contest even with the timid buck, when he is brought to the death-struggle, and has no choice but yielding his life or putting himself upon the defensive, by the aid of his splendid antlers, and with all the courage of despair.

The quantity of game found in Douglas Dale on this occasion was very considerable, for, as already noticed, it was a long time since a hunting upon a great scale had been attempted under the Douglasses themselves, whose misfortunes had commenced, several years before, with those of their country. The English garrison, too, had not sooner judged themselves strong or numerous enough to exercise these valued feudal privileges. In the meantime the game increased considerably. The deer, the wild cattle, and the wild boars, lay near the foot of the mountains, and made frequent irruptions into the lower part of the valley, which in Douglas Dale bears no small resemblance to an oasis, surrounded by tangled woods, and broken moors, occasionally rocky, and showing large tracts of that bleak dominion to which wild creatures gladly escape when pressed by the neighbourhood of man.

As the hunters traversed the spots which separated the field from the wood, there was always a stimulating uncertainty what sort of game was to be found, and the marksman, with his bow ready bent, or his javelin poised, and his good and well-bitted horse thrown upon its haunches, ready for a sudden start, observed watchfully what should rush from the covert, so that, were it deer, boar, wolf, wild cattle, or any other species of game, he might be in readiness.

The wolf, which, on account of its ravages, was the most obnoxious of the beasts of prey, did not, however, supply the degree of diversion which his name promised ; he usually fled far—in some instances many miles— before he took courage to turn to bay, and though for-

E

midable at such moments, destroying both dogs and
men by his terrible bite, yet at other times was rather
despised for his cowardice. The boar, on the other
hand, was a much more irascible and courageous animal.

The wild cattle, the most formidable of all the tenants
of the ancient Caledonian forest, were, however, to the
English cavaliers, by far the most interesting objects
of pursuit. Altogether, the ringing of bugles, the
clattering of horses' hoofs, the lowing and bellowing of
the enraged mountain cattle, the sobs of deer mangled
by throttling dogs, the wild shouts of exultation of
the men,—made a chorus which extended far through
the scene in which it arose, and seemed to threaten
the inhabitants of the valley even in its inmost
recesses.

During the course of the hunting, when a stag or a
boar was expected, one of the wild cattle often came
rushing forward, bearing down the young trees, crashing
the branches in its progress, and in general dispersing
whatever opposition was presented to it by the hunters.
Sir John de Walton was the only one of the chivalry
of the party who individually succeeded in mastering
one of these powerful animals. Like a Spanish tauridor,
he bore down and killed with his lance a ferocious bull ;
two well-grown calves and three kine were also slain,
being unable to carry off the quantity of arrows, javelins,
and other missiles, directed against them by the archers
and drivers ; but many others, in spite of every endeavour to intercept them, escaped to their gloomy haunts
in the remote skirts of the mountain called Cairntable,
with their hides well feathered with those marks of
human enmity.

A large portion of the morning was spent in this way,
until a particular blast from the master of the hunt
announced that he had not forgot the discreet custom
of the repast, which, on such occasions, was provided

for upon a scale proportioned to the multitude who had been convened to attend the sport.

The blast peculiar to the time, assembled the whole party in an open space in a wood, where their numbers had room and accommodation to sit down upon the green turf, the slain game affording a plentiful supply for roasting or broiling, an employment in which the lower class were all immediately engaged ; while puncheons and pipes, placed in readiness, and scientifically opened, supplied Gascoigne wine, and mighty ale, at the pleasure of those who chose to appeal to them.

The knights, whose rank did not admit of interference, were seated by themselves, and ministered to by their squires and pages, to whom such menial services were not accounted disgraceful, but, on the contrary, a proper step of their education. The number of those distinguished persons seated upon the present occasion at the table of dais, as it was called, (in virtue of a canopy of green boughs with which it was overshadowed,) comprehended Sir John de Walton, Sir Aymer de Valence, and some reverend brethren dedicated to the service of Saint Bride, who, though Scottish ecclesiastics, were treated with becoming respect by the English soldiers. One or two Scottish retainers or vavasours, maintaining, perhaps in prudence, a suitable deference to the English knights, sat at the bottom of the table, and as many English archers, peculiarly respected by their superiors, were invited, according to the modern phrase, to the honours of the sitting.

Sir John de Walton sat at the head of the table ; his eye, though it seemed to have no certain object, yet never for a moment remained stationary, but glanced from one countenance to another of the ring formed by his guests, for such they all were, no doubt, though he himself could hardly have told upon what principle

he had issued the invitations ; and even apparently
was at a loss to think what, in one or two cases, had
procured him the honour of their presence.

One person in particular caught De Walton's eye,
as having the air of a redoubted man-at-arms, although
it seemed as if fortune had not of late smiled upon his
enterprises. He was a tall raw-boned man, of an extremely rugged countenance, and his skin, which showed
itself through many a loophole in his dress, exhibited
a complexion which must have endured all the varieties
of an outlawed life ; and akin to one who had, according
to the customary phrase, " ta'en the bent with Robin
Bruce," in other words, occupied the moors with him
as an insurgent. Some such idea certainly crossed
De Walton's mind. Yet the apparent coolness, and
absence of alarm, with which the stranger sat at the
board of an English officer, at the same time being
wholly in his power, had much in it which was irrecon-
cilable with any such suggestion. De Walton, and
several of those about him, had in the course of the day
observed that this tattered cavalier, the most remarkable parts of whose garb and equipments consisted
of an old coat-of-mail and a rusted yet massive partisan
about eight feet long, was possessed of superior
skill in the art of hunting to any individual of their
numerous party. The governor having looked at this
suspicious figure until he had rendered the stranger
aware of the special interest which he attracted, at
length filled a goblet of choice wine, and requested him,
as one of the best pupils of Sir Tristrem who had attended upon the day's chase, to pledge him in a vintage
superior to that supplied to the general company.

" I suppose, however, sir," said De Walton, " you
will have no objections to put off my challenge of a
brimmer, until you can answer my pledge in Gascoigne
wine, which grew in the king's own demesne, was pressed

for his own lip, and is therefore fittest to be emptied
to his majesty's health and prosperity."

" One half of the island of Britain," said the woods-
man, with great composure, " will be of your honour's
opinion ; but as I belong to the other half, even the
choicest liquor in Gascony cannot render that health
acceptable to me."

A murmur of disapprobation ran through the warriors
present ; the priests hung their heads, looked deadly
grave, and muttered their pater-nosters.

" You see, stranger," said De Walton sternly, " that
your speech discomposes the company."

" It may be so," replied the man, in the same blunt
tone ; " and it may happen that there is no harm in
the speech notwithstanding."

" Do you consider that it is made in my presence ? "
answered De Walton.

" Yes, Sir Governor."

" And have you thought what must be the necessary
inference ? " continued De Walton.

" I may form a round guess," answered the stranger,
" what I might have to fear, if your safe conduct and
word of honour, when inviting me to this hunting, were
less trustworthy than I know full well it really is. But
I am your guest—your meat is even now passing my
throat—your cup, filled with right good wine, I have
just now quaffed off—and I would not fear the rankest
Paynim infidel, if we stood in such relation together,
much less an English knight. I tell you, besides, Sir
Knight, you undervalue the wine we have quaffed.
The high flavour and contents of your cup, grow where
it will, give me spirit to tell you one or two circumstances,
which cold cautious sobriety would, in a moment like
this, have left unsaid. You wish, I doubt not, to know
who I am ? My Christian name is Michael—my sur-
name is that of Turnbull, a redoubted clan, to whose

honours, even in the field of hunting or of battle, I have added something. My abode is beneath the mountain of Rubieslaw, by the fair streams of Teviot. You are surprised that I know how to hunt the wild cattle,—I, who have made them my sport from infancy in the lonely forests of Jed and Southdean, and have killed more of them than you or any Englishman in your host ever saw, even if you include the doughty deeds of this day."

The bold borderer made this declaration with the same provoking degree of coolness which predominated in his whole demeanour, and was indeed his principal attribute. His effrontery did not fail to produce its effect upon Sir John de Walton, who instantly called out, " To arms ! to arms !—Secure the spy and traitor ! Ho ! pages and yeomen—William, Anthony, Bend-the-Bow, and Greenleaf—seize the traitor, and bind him with your bowstrings and dog-leashes—bind him, I say, until the blood start from beneath his nails ! "

" Here is a goodly summons ! " said Turnbull, with a sort of horse-laugh. " Were I as sure of being answered by twenty men I could name, there would be small doubt of the upshot of this day."

The archers thickened around the hunter, yet laid no hold on him, none of them being willing to be the first who broke the peace proper to the occasion.

" Tell me," said De Walton, " thou traitor, for what waitest thou here ? "

" Simply and solely," said the Jed forester, " that I may deliver up to the Douglas the castle of his ancestors, and that I may ensure thee, Sir Englishman, the payment of thy deserts, by cutting that very throat which thou makest such a bawling use of."

At the same time, perceiving that the yeomen were crowding behind him to carry their lord's commands into execution so soon as they should be reiterated, the huntsman turned himself short round upon those who appeared about to surprise him, and having, by the suddenness of the action, induced them to step back a pace, he proceeded—" Yes, John de Walton, my purpose was ere now to have put thee to death, as one whom I find in possession of that castle and territory which belong to my master, a knight much more worthy than thyself ; but I know not why I have paused— thou hast given me food when I have hungered for twenty-four hours, I have not therefore had the heart to pay thee at advantage as thou hast deserved.   Begone from this place and country, and take the fair warning of a foe ; thou hast constituted thyself the mortal enemy of this people, and there are those among them who have seldom been injured or defied with impunity. Take no care in searching after me,—it will be in vain, —until I meet thee at a time which will come at my pleasure, not thine.   Push not your inquisition into cruelty, to discover by what means I have deceived you, for it is impossible for you to learn ; and with this friendly advice, look at me and take your leave, for although we shall one day meet, it may be long ere I see you again."

De Walton remained silent, hoping that his prisoner, (for he saw no chance of his escaping,) might, in his communicative humour, drop some more information, and was not desirous to precipitate a fray with which the scene was likely to conclude, unconscious at the same time of the advantage which he thereby gave the daring hunter.

As Turnbull concluded his sentence, he made a sudden spring backwards, which carried him out of the circle formed around him, and before they were aware of his intentions, at once disappeared among the under-wood.

" Seize him—seize him ! " repeated De Walton ;

" let us have him at least at our discretion, unless the earth has actually swallowed him."

This indeed appeared not unlikely, for near the place where Turnbull had made the spring, there yawned a steep ravine, into which he plunged, and descended by the assistance of branches, bushes, and copsewood, until he reached the bottom, where he found some road to the outskirts of the forest, through which he made his escape, leaving the most expert woodsmen among the pursuers totally at fault, and unable to trace his footsteps.

Sir Walter Scott (1771–1832).

From " Castle Dangerous," Chapter VII

The Indian Jugglers

Coming forward and seating himself on the ground in his white dress and tightened turban, the chief of the Indian Jugglers begins with tossing up two brass balls, which is what any of us could do, and concludes with keeping up four at the same time, which is what none of us could do to save our lives, nor if we were to take our whole lives to do it in. Is it then a trifling power we see at work, or is it not something next to miraculous ? It is the utmost stretch of human ingenuity, which nothing but the bending the faculties of body and mind to it from the tenderest infancy with incessant, ever anxious application up to manhood can accomplish or make even a slight approach to. Man, thou art a wonderful animal, and thy ways past finding out ! Thou canst do strange things, but thou turnest them to little account !—To conceive of this effort of extraordinary dexterity distracts the imagination and makes admiration breathless. Yet it costs nothing to the performer, any more than if it were a mere mechanical deception with which he had nothing to do but to watch and laugh at the astonishment of the spectators. A single error of a hair's-breadth, of the smallest conceivable portion of time, would be fatal : the precision of the movements must be like a mathematical truth, their rapidity is like lightning. To catch four balls in succession in less than a second of time, and deliver them back so as to return with seeming consciousness to the hand again ; to make them revolve round him at certain intervals, like the planets in their spheres ; to make them chase one another like sparkles of fire, or shoot up like flowers or meteors ; to throw them behind his back and twine them round his neck like ribbons or like serpents ; to do what appears an impossibility, and to do it with all the ease, the grace, the carelessness imaginable ; to laugh at, to play with the glittering mockeries ; to follow them with his eye as if he could fascinate them with its lambent fire, or as if he had only to see that they kept time with the music on the stage,—there is something in all this which he who does not admire may be quite sure he never really admired anything in the whole course of his life. It is skill surmounting difficulty, and beauty triumphing over skill. It seems as if the difficulty once mastered naturally resolved itself into ease and grace, and as if to be overcome at all, it must be overcome without an effort. The smallest awkwardness or want of pliancy or self-possession would stop the whole process. It is the work of witchcraft, and yet sport for children. Some of the other feats are quite as curious and wonderful, such as the balancing the artificial tree and shooting a bird from each branch through a quill ; though none of them have the elegance or facility of the keeping up of the brass balls. You are in pain for the result, and glad when the experiment is over ; they are not accom-

panied with the same unmixed, unchecked delight as
the former ; and I would not give much to be merely
astonished without being pleased at the same time. As
to the swallowing of the sword, the police ought to
interfere to prevent it. When I saw the Indian Juggler
do the same things before, his feet were bare, and he
had large rings on the toes, which kept turning round
all the time of the performance, as if they moved of
themselves.—The hearing a speech in Parliament
drawled or stammered out by the Honourable Member
or the Noble Lord ; the ringing the changes on their
common-places, which any one could repeat after them
as well as they, stirs me not a jot, shakes not my good
opinion of myself ; but the seeing the Indian Jugglers
does. It makes me ashamed of myself. I ask what
there is that I can do as well as this ? Nothing. What
have I been doing all my life ? Have I been idle, or
have I nothing to show for all my labour and pains ?
Or have I passed my time in pouring words like water
into empty sieves, rolling a stone up a hill and then
down again, trying to prove an argument in the teeth
of facts, and looking for causes in the dark and not
finding them ? Is there no one thing in which I can
challenge competition, that I can bring as an instance
of exact perfection in which others cannot find a flaw ?
The utmost I can pretend to is to write a description
of what this fellow can do. I can write a book : so
can many others who have not even learned to spell.
What abortions are these Essays ! What errors, what
ill-pieced transitions, what crooked reasons, what lame
conclusions ! How little is made out, and that little
how ill ! Yet they are the best I can do. I endeavour
to recollect all I have ever observed or thought upon a
subject, and to express it as nearly as I can. Instead
of writing on four subjects at a time, it is as much as
I can manage to keep the thread of one discourse clear

and unentangled. I have also time on my hands to correct my opinions, and polish my periods; but the one I cannot, and the other I will not do. I am fond of arguing: yet with a good deal of pains and practice it is often as much as I can do to beat my man; though he may be an indifferent hand. A common fencer would disarm his adversary in the twinkling of an eye, unless he were a professor like himself. A stroke of wit will sometimes produce this effect, but there is no such power or superiority in sense or reasoning. There is no complete mastery of execution to be shown there; and you hardly know the professor from the impudent pretender or the mere clown.[1]

I have always had this feeling of the inefficacy and slow progress of intellectual compared to mechanical excellence, and it has always made me somewhat dissatisfied. It is a great many years since I saw Richer, the famous rope-dancer, perform at Sadler's Wells. He was matchless in his art, and added to his extraordinary skill exquisite ease, and unaffected, natural grace. I was at that time employed in copying a half-length picture of Sir Joshua Reynolds's; and it put me out of conceit with it. How ill this part was made out in the drawing! How heavy, how slovenly this other was painted! I could not help saying to myself, " If the

---

[1] The celebrated Peter Pindar (Dr. Wolcot) first discovered and brought out the talents of the late Mr. Opie the painter. He was a poor Cornish boy, and was out at work in the fields when the poet went in search of him. " Well, my lad, can you go and bring me your very best picture ? " The other flew like lightning, and soon came back with what he considered as his masterpiece. The stranger looked at it, and the young artist, after waiting for some time without his giving any opinion, at length exclaimed eagerly, " Well, what do you think of it ? " " Think of it ? " said Wolcot ; " why, I think you ought to be ashamed of it—that you, who might do so well, do no better ! " The same answer would have applied to this artist's latest performances, that had been suggested by one of his earliest efforts.

rope-dancer had performed his task in this manner, leaving so many gaps and botches in his work, he would have broken his neck long ago ; I should never have seen that vigorous elasticity of nerve and precision of movement ! "—Is it, then, so easy an undertaking (comparatively) to dance on a tight-rope ? Let any one who thinks so get up and try. There is the thing. It is that which at first we cannot do at all which in the end is done to such perfection. To account for this in some degree, I might observe that mechanical dexterity is confined to doing some one particular thing, which you can repeat as often as you please, in which you know whether you succeed or fail, and where the point of perfection consists in succeeding in a given undertaking.—In mechanical efforts you improve by perpetual practice, and you do so infallibly, because the object to be attained is not a matter of taste or fancy or opinion, but of actual experiment, in which you must either do the thing or not do it. If a man is put to aim at a mark with a bow and arrow, he must hit it or miss it, that's certain. He cannot deceive himself, and go on shooting wide or falling short, and still fancy that he is making progress. The distinction between right and wrong, between true and false, is here palpable ; and he must either correct his aim or persevere in his error with his eyes open, for which there is neither excuse nor temptation. If a man is learning to dance on a rope, if he does not mind what he is about he will break his neck. After that it will be in vain for him to argue that he did not make a false step. His situation is not like that of Goldsmith's pedagogue :—

> In argument they own'd his wondrous skill,
> And e'en though vanquish'd, he could argue still.

Danger is a good teacher, and makes apt scholars. So are disgrace, defeat, exposure to immediate scorn and laughter. There is no opportunity in such cases for self-delusion, no idling time away, no being off your guard (or you must take the consequences)—neither is there any room for humour or caprice or prejudice. If the Indian Juggler were to play tricks in throwing up the three case-knives, which keep their positions like the leaves of a crocus in the air, he would cut his fingers. I can make a very bad antithesis without cutting my fingers. The tact of style is more ambiguous than that of double-edged instruments. If the Juggler were told that by flinging himself under the wheels of the Juggernaut, when the idol issues forth on a gaudy day, he would immediately be transported into Paradise, he might believe it, and nobody could disprove it. So the Brahmins may say what they please on that subject, may build up dogmas and mysteries without end, and not be detected ; but their ingenious countryman cannot persuade the frequenters of the Olympic Theatre that he performs a number of astonishing feats without actually giving proofs of what he says.—There is, then, in this sort of manual dexterity, first a gradual aptitude acquired to a given exertion of muscular power, from constant repetition, and in the next place, an exact knowledge how much is still wanting and necessary to be supplied. The obvious test is to increase the effort or nicety of the operation, and still to find it come true. The muscles ply instinctively to the dictates of habit. Certain movements and impressions of the hand and eye, having been repeated together an infinite number of times, are unconsciously but unavoidably cemented into closer and closer union ; the limbs require little more than to be put in motion for them to follow a regular track with ease and certainty ; so that the mere intention of the will acts mathematically like touching the spring of a machine, and you come with Locksley in *Ivanhoe*, in shooting at a mark, " to allow for the wind."

Further, what is meant by perfection in mechanical exercises is the performing certain feats to a uniform nicety, that is, in fact, undertaking no more than you can perform. You task yourself, the limit you fix is optional, and no more than human industry and skill can attain to ; but you have no abstract, independent standard of difficulty or excellence (other than the extent of your own powers). Thus he who can keep up four brass balls does this *to perfection* ; but he cannot keep up five at the same instant, and would fail every time he attempted it. That is, the mechanical performer undertakes to emulate himself, not to equal another.[1] But the artist undertakes to imitate another, or to do what Nature has done, and this it appears is more diffi- cult, viz. to copy what she has set before us in the face of nature or " human face divine," entire and without a blemish, than to keep up four brass balls at the same instant, for the one is done by the power of human skill and industry, and the other never was nor will be. Upon the whole, therefore, I have more respect for Reynolds than I have for Richer ; for, happen how it will, there have been more people in the world who could dance on a rope like the one than who could paint like Sir Joshua. The latter was but a bungler in his profession to the other, it is true ; but then he had a harder taskmaster to obey, whose will was more way- ward and obscure, and whose instructions it was more difficult to practise. You can put a child apprentice to a tumbler or rope-dancer with a comfortable prospect of success, if they are but sound of wind and limb ; but you cannot do the same thing in painting. The odds are a million to one. You may make indeed as many Haydons and H——s as you put into that sort of machine, but not one Reynolds amongst them all, with

[1] If two persons play against each other at any game, one of them necessarily fails.

his grace, his grandeur, his blandness of gusto, "in tones and gestures hit," unless you could make the man over again. To snatch this grace beyond the reach of art is then the height of art—where fine art begins, and where mechanical skill ends. The soft suffusion of the soul, the speechless breathing eloquence, the looks "commercing with the skies," the ever-shifting forms of an eternal principle, that which is seen but for a moment, but dwells in the heart always, and is only seized as it passes by strong and secret sympathy, must be taught by nature and genius, not by rules or study. It is suggested by feeling, not by laborious microscopic inspection; in seeking for it without, we lose the harmonious clue to it within; and in aiming to grasp the substance, we let the very spirit of art evaporate. In a word, the objects of fine art are not the objects of sight but as these last are the objects of taste and imagination, that is, as they appeal to the sense of beauty, of pleasure, and of power in the human breast, and are explained by that finer sense, and revealed in their inner structure to the eye in return. Nature is also a language. Objects, like words, have a meaning; and the true artist is the interpreter of this language, which he can only do by knowing its application to a thousand other objects in a thousand other situations. Thus the eye is too blind a guide of itself to distinguish between the warm or cold tone of a deep-blue sky; but another sense acts as a monitor to it and does not err. The colour of the leaves in autumn would be nothing without the feeling that accompanies it; but it is that feeling that stamps them on the canvas, faded, seared, blighted, shrinking from the winter's flaw, and makes the sight as true as touch.—

And visions, as poetic eyes avow,
Cling to each leaf and hang on every bough.

The more ethereal, evanescent, more refined and sublime part of art is the seeing nature through the medium of sentiment and passion, as each object is a symbol of the affections and a link in the chain of our endless being. But the unravelling this mysterious web of thought and feeling is alone in the Muse's gift, namely, in the power of that trembling sensibility which is awake to every change and every modification of its ever-varying impressions, that

> Thrills in each nerve, and lives along the line.

This power is indifferently called genius, imagination, feeling, taste ; but the manner in which it acts upon the mind can neither be defined by abstract rules, as is the case in science, nor verified by continual, unvarying experiments, as is the case in mechanical performances. The mechanical excellence of the Dutch painters in colouring and handling is that which comes the nearest in fine art to the perfection of certain manual exhibitions of skill. The truth of the effect and the facility with which it is produced are equally admirable. Up to a certain point everything is faultless. The hand and eye have done their part. There is only a want of taste and genius. It is after we enter upon that enchanted ground that the human mind begins to droop and flag as in a strange road, or in a thick mist, benighted and making little way with many attempts and many failures, and that the best of us only escape with half a triumph. The undefined and the imaginary are the regions that we must pass like Satan, difficult and doubtful, " half flying, half on foot." The object in sense is a positive thing, and execution comes with practice.

Cleverness is a certain *knack* or aptitude at doing certain things, which depend more on a particular adroitness and off-hand readiness than on force or perseverance, such as making puns, making epigrams, making extempore verses, mimicking the company, mimicking a style, etc. Cleverness is either liveliness and smartness, or something answering to *sleight of hand*, like letting a glass fall sideways off a table, or else a trick, like knowing the secret spring of a watch. Accomplishments are certain external graces, which are to be learned from others, and which are easily displayed to the admiration of the beholder, viz. dancing, riding, fencing, music, and so on. These ornamental acquirements are only proper to those who are at ease in mind and fortune. I know an individual who, if he had been born to an estate of five thousand a year, would have been the most accomplished gentleman of the age. He would have been the delight and envy of the circle in which he moved—would have graced by his manners the liberality flowing from the openness of his heart, would have laughed with the women, have argued with the men, have said good things and written agreeable ones, have taken a hand at piquet or the lead at the harpsichord, and have set and sung his own verses— *nugæ canoræ*—with tenderness and spirit ; a Rochester without the vice, a modern Surrey. As it is, all these capabilities of excellence stand in his way. He is too versatile for a professional man, not dull enough for a political drudge, too gay to be happy, too thoughtless to be rich. He wants the enthusiasm of the poet, the severity of the prose-writer, and the application of the man of business. Talent is the capacity of doing anything that depends on application and industry, such as writing a criticism, making a speech, studying the law. Talent differs from genius as voluntary differs from involuntary power. Ingenuity is genius in trifles ; greatness is genius in undertakings of much pith and moment. A clever or ingenious man is one who can do anything well, whether it is worth doing or not ; a

F

great man is one who can do that which when done is
of the highest importance. Themistocles said he could
not play on the flute, but that he could make of a small
city a great one. This gives one a pretty good idea of
the distinction in question.

Greatness is great power, producing great effects. It
is not enough that a man has great power in himself ;
he must show it to all the world in a way that cannot
be hid or gainsaid. He must fill up a certain idea in
the public mind. I have no other notion of greatness
than this twofold definition, great results springing
from great inherent energy. The great in visible objects
has relation to that which extends over space ; the
great in mental ones has to do with space and time.
No man is truly great who is great only in his lifetime.
The test of greatness is the page of history. Nothing
can be said to be great that has a distinct limit, or that
borders on something evidently greater than itself.
Besides, what is short-lived and pampered into mere
notoriety is of a gross and vulgar quality in itself. A
Lord Mayor is hardly a great man. A city orator or
patriot of the day only show, by reaching the height of
their wishes, the distance they are at from any true
ambition. Popularity is neither fame nor greatness.
A king (as such) is not a great man. He has great
power, but it is not his own. He merely wields the
lever of the state, which a child, an idiot, or a madman
can do. It is the office, not the man we gaze at. Any
one else in the same situation would be just as much
an object of abject curiosity. We laugh at the country
girl who having seen a king expressed her disappointment by saying, " Why, he is only a man ! " Yet,
knowing this, we run to see a king as if he was something more than a man.—To display the greatest powers,
unless they are applied to great purposes, makes nothing for the character of greatness. To throw a barley-

corn through the eye of a needle, to multiply nine figures
by nine in the memory, argues definite dexterity of
body and capacity of mind, but nothing comes of either.
There is a surprising power at work, but the effects
are not proportionate, or such as take hold of the imagination. To impress the idea of power on others, they
must be made in some way to feel it. It must be communicated to their understandings in the shape of an
increase of knowledge, or it must subdue and overawe
them by subjecting their wills. Admiration to be solid
and lasting must be founded on proofs from which we
have no means of escaping ; it is neither a slight nor
a voluntary gift. A mathematician who solves a profound problem, a poet who creates an image of beauty
in the mind that was not there before, imparts knowledge and power to others, in which his greatness and
his fame consists, and on which it reposes. Jedediah
Buxton will be forgotten ; but Napier's bones will live.
Lawgivers, philosophers, founders of religion, conquerors
and heroes, inventors and great geniuses in arts and
sciences, are great men, for they are great public bene-
factors, or formidable scourges to mankind. Among
ourselves, Shakespeare, Newton, Bacon, Milton, Cromwell, were great men, for they showed great power by
acts and thoughts, which have not yet been consigned
to oblivion. They must needs be men of lofty stature,
whose shadows lengthen out to remote posterity. A
great farce-writer may be a great man ; for Molière
was but a great farce-writer. In my mind, the author
of *Don Quixote* was a great man. So have there been
many others. A great chess-player is not a great man,
for he leaves the world as he found it. No act terminating in itself constitutes greatness. This will apply to
all displays of power or trials of skill which are confined
to the momentary, individual effort, and construct no
permanent image or trophy of themselves without them,

Is not an actor then a great man, because " he dies and
leaves the world no copy " ?   I must make an exception
for Mrs. Siddons, or else give up my definition of greatness for her sake.   A man at the top of his profession
is not therefore a great man.   He is great in his way,
but that is all, unless he shows the marks of a great
moving intellect, so that we trace the master-mind,
and can sympathize with the springs that urge him on.
The rest is but a craft or *mystery*.   John Hunter was a
great man—*that* any one might see without the smallest
skill in surgery.   His style and manner showed the man.
He would set about cutting up the carcass of a whale
with the same greatness of gusto that Michael Angelo
would have hewn a block of marble.   Lord Nelson was
a great naval commander ; but for myself, I have not
much opinion of a seafaring life.   Sir Humphrey Davy
is a great chemist, but I am not sure that he is a great
man.   I am not a bit the wiser for any of his discoveries,
nor I never met with any one that was.   But it is in
the nature of greatness to propagate an idea of itself,
as wave impels wave, circle without circle.   It is a
contradiction in terms for a coxcomb to be a great man.
A really great man has always an idea of something
greater than himself.   I have observed that certain
sectaries and polemical writers have no higher compliment to pay their most shining lights than to say that,
" Such a one was a considerable man in his day."   Some
new elucidation of a text sets aside the authority of
the old interpretation, and a " great scholar's memory
outlives him half a century," at the utmost.   A rich
man is not a great man, except to his dependants and
his steward,   A lord is a great man in the idea we have
of his ancestry, and probably of himself, if we know
nothing of him but his title.   I have heard a story of
two bishops, one of whom said (speaking of St. Peter's
at Rome) that when he first entered it, he was rather

awe-struck, but that as he walked up it, his mind seemed
to swell and dilate with it, and at last to fill the whole
building : the other said that as he saw more of it, he
appeared to himself to grow less and less every step he
took, and in the end to dwindle into nothing. This
was in some respects a striking picture of a great and
little mind ; for greatness sympathizes with greatness,
and littleness shrinks into itself. The one might have
become a Wolsey ; the other was only fit to become a
Mendicant Friar—or there might have been court reasons
for making him a bishop. The French have to me a
character of littleness in all about them ; but they have
produced three great men that belong to every country,
Molière, Rabelais, and Montaigne.

To return from this digression, and conclude the
Essay. A singular instance of manual dexterity was
shown in the person of the late John Cavanagh, whom
I have several times seen. His death was celebrated
at the time in an article in the *Examiner* newspaper
(Feb. 7, 1819), written apparently between jest and
earnest ; but as it is *pat* to our purpose, and falls in
with my own way of considering such subjects, I shall
here take leave to quote it :—

" Died at his house in Burbage Street, St. Giles's,
John Cavanagh, the famous hand fives-player. When
a person dies who does any one thing better than any
one else in the world, which so many others are trying
to do well, it leaves a gap in society. It is not likely
that any one will now see the game of fives played in
its perfection for many years to come—for Cavanagh is
dead, and has not left his peer behind him. It may
be said that there are things of more importance than
striking a ball against a wall—there are things, indeed,
that make more noise and do as little good, such as
making war and peace, making speeches and answering
them, making verses and blotting them, making money

and throwing it away. But the game of fives is what no one despises who has ever played at it. It is the finest exercise for the body, and the best relaxation for the mind. The Roman poet said that ' Care mounted behind the horseman and stuck to his skirts.' But this remark would not have applied to the fives-player. He who takes to playing at fives is twice young. He feels neither the past nor future ' in the instant.' Debts, taxes, ' domestic treason, foreign levy, nothing can touch him further.' He has no other wish, no other thought, from the moment the game begins, but that of striking the ball, of placing it, of *making* it ! This Cavanagh was sure to do. Whenever he touched the ball there was an end of the chase. His eye was certain, his hand fatal, his presence of mind complete. He could do what he pleased, and he always knew exactly what to do. He saw the whole game, and played it ; took instant advantage of his adversary's weakness, and recovered balls, as if by a miracle and from sudden thought, that every one gave for lost. He had equal power and skill, quickness and judgment. He could either outwit his antagonist by finesse, or beat him by main strength. Sometimes, when he seemed preparing to send the ball with the full swing of his arm, he would by a slight turn of his wrist drop it within an inch of the line. In general, the ball came from his hand, as if from a racket, in a straight, horizontal line ; so that it was in vain to attempt to overtake or stop it. As it was said of a great orator that he never was at a loss for a word, and for the properest word, so Cavanagh always could tell the degree of force necessary to be given to a ball, and the precise direction in which it should be sent. He did his work with the greatest ease ; never took more pains than was necessary ; and while others were fagging themselves to death, was as cool and collected as if he had just entered

the court. His style of play was as remarkable as his
power of execution. He had no affectation, no trifling.
He did not throw away the game to show off an attitude
or try an experiment. He was a fine, sensible, manly
player, who did what he could, but that was more than
any one else could even affect to do. His blows were
not undecided and ineffectual—lumbering like Mr.
Wordsworth's epic poetry, nor wavering like Mr. Coleridge's lyric prose, nor short of the mark like Mr. Brough-
am's speeches, nor wide of it like Mr. Canning's wit,
nor foul like the *Quarterly*, nor *let* balls like the *Edinburgh
Review*. Cobbett and Junius together would have made
a Cavanagh. He was the best *up-hill* player in the
world ; even when his adversary was fourteen, he would
play on the same or better, and as he never flung away
the game through carelessness and conceit, he never
gave it up through laziness or want of heart. The
only peculiarity of his play was that he never *volleyed*,
but let the balls hop ; but if they rose an inch from
the ground he never missed having them. There was
not only nobody equal, but nobody second to him. It
is supposed that he could give any other player half the
game, or beat them with his left hand. His service
was tremendous. He once played Woodward and
Meredith together (two of the best players in England)
in the Fives-court, St. Martin's Street, and made seven-
and-twenty aces following by services alone—a thing
unheard of. He another time played Peru, who was
considered a first-rate fives-player, a match of the best
out of five games, and in the three first games, which
of course decided the match, Peru got only one ace.
Cavanagh was an Irishman by birth, and a house-painter
by profession. He had once laid aside his working-
dress, and walked up, in his smartest clothes, to the
Rosemary Branch to have an afternoon's pleasure. A
person accosted him, and asked him if he would have a

game. So they agreed to play for half a crown a game
and a bottle of cider. The first game began—it was
seven, eight, ten, thirteen, fourteen, all. Cavanagh
won it. The next was the same. They played on,
and each game was hardly contested. 'There,' said
the unconscious fives-player, 'there was a stroke that
Cavanagh could not take : I never played better in my
life, and yet I can't win a game. I don't know how it
is !' However, they played on, Cavanagh winning
every game, and the bystanders drinking the cider and
laughing all the time. In the twelfth game, when
Cavanagh was only four, and the stranger thirteen, a
person came in and said, 'What ! are you here, Cavanagh ? ' The words were no sooner pronounced than
the astonished player let the ball drop from his hand,
and saying, 'What ! have I been breaking my heart
all this time to beat Cavanagh ? 'refused to make another
effort. 'And yet, I give you my word,' said Cavanagh,
telling the story with some triumph, 'I played all the
while with my clenched fist.' He used frequently to
play matches at Copenhagen House for wagers and
dinners. The wall against which they play is the same
that supports the kitchen-chimney, and when the wall
resounded louder than usual, the cooks exclaimed,
' Those are the Irishman's balls,' and the joints trembled
on the spit ! Goldsmith consoled himself that there
were places where he too was admired : and Cavanagh
was the admiration of all the fives-courts where he ever
played. Mr. Powell, when he played matches in the
court in St. Martin's Street, used to fill his gallery at
half a crown a head with amateurs and admirers of
talent in whatever department it is shown. He could
not have shown himself in any ground in England but
he would have been immediately surrounded with
inquisitive gazers, trying to find out in what part of
his frame his unrivalled skill lay, as politicians wonder

to see the balance of Europe suspended in Lord Castle-
reagh's face, and admire the trophies of the British
Navy lurking under Mr. Croker's hanging brow. Now
Cavanagh was as good-looking a man as the Noble
Lord, and much better looking than the Right Hon.
Secretary. He had a clear, open countenance, and did
not look sideways or down, like Mr. Murray the book-
seller. He was a young fellow of sense, humour, and
courage. He once had a quarrel with a waterman at
Hungerford Stairs, and, they say, served him out in
great style. In a word, there are hundreds at this day
who cannot mention his name without admiration, as
the best fives-player that perhaps ever lived (the greatest
excellence of which they have any notion); and the
noisy shout of the ring happily stood him in stead of
the unheard voice of posterity!—The only person who
seems to have excelled as much in another way as
Cavanagh did in his was the late John Davies, the
racket-player. It was remarked of him that he did
not seem to follow the ball, but the ball seemed to
follow him. Give him a foot of wall, and he was sure
to make the ball. The four best racket-players of that
day were Jack Spines, Jem Harding, Armitage, and
Church. Davies could give any one of these two hands
a time, that is, half the game, and each of these, at
their best, could give the best player now in London
the same odds. Such are the gradations in all exertions
of human skill and art. He once played four capital
players together, and beat them. He was also a first-
rate tennis-player, and an excellent fives-player. In
the Fleet or King's Bench he would have stood against
Powell, who was reckoned the best open-ground player
of his time. This last-mentioned player is at present
the keeper of the Fives-court, and we might recommend
to him for a motto over his door, ' Who enters here,
forgets himself, his country, and his friends.' And the

best of it is, that by the calculation of the odds, none
of the three are worth remembering ! Cavanagh died
from the bursting of a blood-vessel, which prevented
him from playing for the last two or three years. This,
he was often heard to say, he thought hard upon him.
He was fast recovering, however, when he was suddenly
carried off, to the regret of all who knew him. As Mr.
Peel made it a qualification of the present Speaker,
Mr. Manners Sutton, that he was an excellent moral
character, so Jack Cavanagh was a zealous Catholic,
and could not be persuaded to eat meat on a Friday,
the day on which he died. We have paid this willing
tribute to his memory.

> Let no rude hand deface it,
> And his forlorn ' *Hic Jacet.*' "

William Hazlitt (1778–1830).

The Grey Champion

There was once a time when New England groaned
under the actual pressure of heavier wrongs than those
threatened ones which brought on the Revolution.
James II, the bigoted successor of Charles the Volup-
tuous, had annulled the charters of all the colonies, and
sent a harsh and unprincipled soldier to take away our
liberties and endanger our religion. The administra-
tion of Sir Edmund Andros lacked scarcely a single
characteristic of tyranny : a Governor and Council,
holding office from the King, and wholly independent
of the country ; laws made and taxes levied without
concurrence of the people, immediate or by their representatives ; the rights of private citizens violated, and
the titles of all landed property declared void ; the
voice of complaint stifled by restrictions on the press ;

and, finally, disaffection overawed by the first band of
mercenary troops that ever marched on our free soil.
For two years our ancestors were kept in sullen submission, by that filial love which had invariably secured
their allegiance to the mother country, whether its head
chanced to be a Parliament, Protector, or Popish Monarch. Till these evil times, however, such allegiance
had been merely nominal, and the colonists had ruled
themselves, enjoying far more freedom than is even
yet the privilege of the native subjects of Great Britain.

At length, a rumour reached our shores that the
Prince of Orange had ventured on an enterprise, the
success of which would be the triumph of civil and
religious rights and the salvation of New England. It
was but a doubtful whisper ; it might be false, or the
attempt might fail ; and, in either case, the man that
stirred against King James would lose his head. Still
the intelligence produced a marked effect. The people
smiled mysteriously in the streets, and threw bold
glances at their oppressors ; while, far and wide, there
was a subdued and silent agitation, as if the slightest
signal would rouse the whole land from its sluggish
despondency. Aware of their danger, the rulers resolved to avert it by an imposing display of strength,
and perhaps to confirm their despotism by yet harsher
measures. One afternoon in April, 1689, Sir Edmund
Andros and his favourite councillors, being warm with
wine, assembled the red-coats of the Governor's Guard,
and made their appearance in the streets of Boston.
The sun was near setting when the march commenced.

The roll of the drum, at that unquiet crisis, seemed
to go through the streets, less as the martial music of
the soldiers, than as a muster call to the inhabitants
themselves A multitude, by various avenues, assembled in King Street, which was destined to be the scene,
nearly a century afterwards, of another encounter

between the troops of Britain and a people struggling against her tyranny. Though more than sixty years had elapsed since the Pilgrims came, this crowd of their descendants still showed the strong and sombre features of their character, perhaps more strikingly in such a stern emergency than on happier occasions. There were the sober garb, the general severity of mien, the gloomy but undismayed expression, the scriptural forms of speech, and the confidence in Heaven's blessing on a righteous cause, which would have marked a band of the original Puritans, when threatened by some peril of the wilderness. Indeed, it was not yet time for the old spirit to be extinct; since there were men in the street, that day, who had worshipped there beneath the trees, before a house was reared to the God for whom they had become exiles. Old soldiers of the Parliament were here, too, smiling grimly at the thought, that their aged arms might strike another blow against the house of Stuart. Here, also, were the veterans of King Philip's war, who had burned villages and slaughtered young and old, with pious fierceness, while the godly souls throughout the land were helping them with prayer. Several ministers were scattered among the crowd, which, unlike all other mobs, regarded them with such reverence, as if there were sanctity in their very garments. These holy men exerted their influence to quiet the people, but not to disperse them. Meantime, the purpose of the Governor, in disturbing the peace of the town, at a period when the slightest commotion might throw the country into a ferment, was almost the universal subject of inquiry, and variously explained.

" Satan will strike his master-stroke presently," cried some, " because he knoweth that his time is short. All our godly pastors are to be dragged to prison! We shall see them at a Smithfield fire in King Street ! "

Hereupon the people of each parish gathered closer

round their minister, who looked calmly upwards and assumed a more apostolic dignity, as well befitted a candidate for the highest honour of his profession, the crown of martyrdom. It was actually fancied, at that period, that New England might have a John Rogers of her own, to take the place of that worthy in the Primer.

" The Pope of Rome has given orders for a new St. Bartholomew ! " cried others. " We are to be massacred, man and male child ! "

Neither was this rumour wholly discredited, although the wiser class believed the Governor's object somewhat less atrocious. His predecessor under the old charter, Bradstreet, a venerable companion of the first settlers, was known to be in town. There were grounds for conjecturing that Sir Edmund Andros intended, at once, to strike terror, by a parade of military force, and to confound the opposite faction, by possessing himself of their chief.

" Stand firm for the old charter, Governor ! " shouted the crowd, seizing upon the idea. " The good old Governor Bradstreet ! "

While this cry was at the loudest, the people were surprised by the well-known figure of Governor Bradstreet himself, a patriarch of nearly ninety, who appeared on the elevated steps of a door, and, with characteristic mildness, besought them to submit to the constituted authorities.

" My children," concluded this venerable person, " do nothing rashly. Cry not aloud, but pray for the welfare of New England, and expect patiently what the Lord will do in this matter ! "

The event was soon to be decided. All this time, the roll of the drum had been approaching through Cornhill, louder and deeper, till with reverberations from house to house, and the regular tramp of martial footsteps, it burst into the street. A double rank of soldiers made their appearance, occupying the whole breadth of the passage, with shouldered matchlocks, and matches burning, so as to present a row of fires in the dusk. Their steady march was like the progress of a machine, that would roll irresistibly over everything in its way. Next, moving slowly, with a confused clatter of hoofs on the pavement, rode a party of mounted gentlemen, the central figure being Sir Edmund Andros, elderly, but erect and soldier-like. Those around him were his favourite councillors, and the bitterest foes of New England. At his right hand rode Edward Randolph, our arch-enemy, that " blasted wretch," as Cotton Mather calls him, who achieved the downfall of our ancient government, and was followed with a sensible curse, through life and to his grave. On the other side was Bullivant, scattering jests and mockery as he rode along. Dudley came behind, with a downcast look, dreading, as well he might, to meet the indignant gaze of the people, who beheld him, their only countryman by birth, among the oppressors of his native land. The captain of a frigate in the harbour, and two or three civil officers under the Crown, were also there. But the figure which most attracted the public eye, and stirred up the deepest feeling, was the Episcopal clergyman of King's Chapel, riding haughtily among the magistrates in his priestly vestments, the fitting representative of prelacy and persecution, the union of church and state, and all those abominations which had driven the Puritans to the wilderness. Another guard of soldiers, in double rank, brought up the rear.

The whole scene was a picture of the condition of New England, and its moral, the deformity of any government that does not grow out of the nature of things and the character of the people. On one side the religious multitude. with their sad visages and dark attire, and on the other, the group of despotic rulers, with the High Churchman in the midst, and here and there a crucifix at their bosoms, all magnificently clad, flushed with wine, proud of unjust authority, and scoffing at the universal groan. And the mercenary soldiers, waiting but the word to deluge the street with blood, showed the only means by which obedience could be secured.

" O Lord of Hosts," cried a voice among the crowd, " provide a Champion for Thy people ! "

This ejaculation was loudly uttered, and served as a herald's cry, to introduce a remarkable personage. The crowd had rolled back, and were now huddled together nearly at the extremity of the street, while the soldiers had advanced no more than a third of its length. The intervening space was empty—a paved solitude, between lofty edifices, which threw almost a twilight shadow over it. Suddenly, there was seen the figure of an ancient man, who seemed to have emerged from among the people, and was walking by himself along the centre of the street, to confront the armed band. He wore the old Puritan dress, a dark cloak and a steeple-crowned hat, in the fashion of at least fifty years before, with a heavy sword upon his thigh, but a staff in his hand to assist the tremulous gait of age.

When at some distance from the multitude, the old man turned slowly round, displaying a face of antique majesty, rendered doubly venerable by the hoary beard that descended on his breast. He made a gesture at once of encouragement and warning, then turned again, and resumed his way.

" Who is this grey patriarch ? " asked the young men of their sires.

" Who is this venerable brother ? " asked the old men among themselves.

But none could make reply. The fathers of the

people, those of fourscore years and upwards, were disturbed, deeming it strange that they should forget one
of such evident authority, whom they must have known
in their early days, the associates of Winthrop, and all
the old councillors, giving laws, and making prayers,
and leading them against the savage. The elderly men
ought to have remembered him, too, with locks as grey
in their youth, as their own were now. And the young!
How could he have passed so utterly from their memories
—that hoary sire, the relic of long-departed times,
whose awful benediction had surely been bestowed on
their uncovered heads in childhood?

" Whence did he come? What is his purpose? Who
can this old man be? " whispered the wondering crowd.

Meanwhile, the venerable stranger, staff in hand, was
pursuing his solitary walk along the centre of the street.
As he drew near the advancing soldiers, and as the roll
of the drum came full upon his ear, the old man raised
himself to a loftier mien, while the decrepitude of age
seemed to fall from his shoulders, leaving him in grey
but unbroken dignity. Now, he marched onward with
a warrior's step, keeping time to the military music.
Thus the aged form advanced on one side, and the whole
parade of soldiers and magistrates on the other, till,
when scarcely twenty yards remained between, the old
man grasped his staff by the middle, and held it before
him like a leader's truncheon.

" Stand! " cried he.

The eye, the face, and attitude of command; the
solemn, yet warlike peal of that voice, fit either to rule
a host in the battle field or be raised to God in prayer,
were irresistible. At the old man's word and outstretched arm, the roll of the drum was hushed at once,
and the advancing line stood still. A tremulous enthusiasm seized upon the multitude. That stately form,
combining the leader and the saint, so grey, so dimly

seen, in such an ancient garb, could only belong to some old champion of the righteous cause, whom the oppressor's drum had summoned from his grave. They raised a shout of awe and exultation, and looked for the deliverance of New England.

The Governor, and the gentlemen of his party, perceiving themselves brought to an unexpected stand, rode hastily forward, as if they would have pressed their snorting and affrighted horses right against the hoary apparition. He, however, blenched not a step, but glancing his severe eye round the group, which half encompassed him, at last bent it sternly on Sir Edmund Andros. One would have thought that the dark old man was chief ruler there, and that the Governor and Council, with soldiers at their back, representing the whole power and authority of the Crown, had no alternative but obedience.

"What does this old fellow here?" cried Edward Randolph, fiercely. "On, Sir Edmund! Bid the soldiers forward, and give the dotard the same choice that you give all his countrymen—to stand aside or be trampled on!"

"Nay, nay, let us show respect to the good grandsire," said Bullivant, laughing. "See you not, he is some old round-headed dignitary, who hath lain asleep these thirty years, and knows nothing of the change of times? Doubtless, he thinks to put us down with a proclamation in Old Noll's name!"

"Are you mad, old man?" demanded Sir Edmund Andros, in loud and harsh tones. "How dare you stay the march of King James's Governor?"

"I have stayed the march of a King himself, ere now," replied the grey figure, with stern composure. "I am here, Sir Governor, because the cry of an oppressed people hath disturbed me in my secret place; and beseeching this favour earnestly of the Lord, it was vouchsafed me to appear once again on earth, in the good old cause of His saints. And what speak ye of James ? There is no longer a Popish tyrant on the throne of England, and by to-morrow noon, his name shall be a byword in this very street, where ye would make it a word of terror. Back, thou that wast a Governor, back ! With this night thy power is ended —to-morrow the prison !—back lest I foretell the scaffold ! "

The people had been drawing nearer and nearer, and drinking in the words of their champion, who spoke in accents long disused, like one unaccustomed to converse, except with the dead of many years ago. But his voice stirred their souls. They confronted the soldiers, not wholly without arms, and ready to convert the very stones of the street into deadly weapons. Sir Edmund Andros looked at the old man ; then he cast his hard and cruel eye over the multitude, and beheld them burning with that lurid wrath, so difficult to kindle or to quench ; and again he fixed his gaze on the aged form, which stood obscurely in an open space, where neither friend nor foe had thrust himself. What were his thoughts, he uttered no word which might discover. But whether the oppressor were overawed by the Grey Champion's look, or perceived his peril in the threatening attitude of the people, it is certain that he gave back, and ordered his soldiers to commence a slow and guarded retreat. Before another sunset, the Governor, and all that rode so proudly with him, were prisoners, and long ere it was known that James had abdicated, King William was proclaimed throughout New England.

But where was the Grey Champion ? Some reported, that when the troops had gone from King Street, and the people were thronging tumultuously in their rear, Bradstreet, the aged Governor, was seen to embrace a form more aged than his own. Others soberly affirmed,

that while they marvelled at the venerable grandeur of
his aspect, the old man had faded from their eyes,
melting slowly into the hues of twilight, till, where he
stood, there was an empty space. But all agreed that
the hoary shape was gone. The men of that generation
watched for his reappearance, in sunshine and in twilight,
but never saw him more, nor knew when his funeral
passed, nor where his gravestone was.

And who was the Grey Champion? Perhaps his
name might be found in the records of that stern Court
of Justice which passed a sentence, too mighty for the
age, but glorious in all after times, for its humbling
lesson to the monarch and its high example to the
subject. I have heard, that whenever the descendants
of the Puritans are to show the spirit of their sires, the
old man appears again. When eighty years had passed,
he walked once more in King Street. Five years later,
in the twilight of an April morning, he stood on the
green, beside the meeting-house, at Lexington, where
now the obelisk of granite, with a slab of slate inlaid,
commemorates the first fallen of the Revolution. And
when our fathers were toiling at the breastwork on
Bunker's Hill, all through that night the old warrior
walked his rounds. Long, long may it be ere he comes
again! His hour is one of darkness, and adversity,
and peril. But should domestic tyranny oppress us, or
the invader's step pollute our soil, still may the Grey
Champion come ; for he is the type of New England's
hereditary spirit : and his shadowy march, on the eve
of danger, must ever be the pledge that New England's
sons will vindicate their ancestry.

Nathaniel Hawthorne (1804–1864).

A Chapter on Hats

We know not what will be thought of our taste in so important a matter, but we must confess we are not fond of a new hat. There is a certain insolence about it : it seems to value itself upon its finished appearance, and to presume upon our liking before we are acquainted with it. In the first place, it comes home more like a marmot or some other living creature, than a manufacture. It is boxed up, and wrapt in silver paper, and brought delicately. It is as sleek as a lap-dog. Then we are to take it out as nicely, and people are to wonder how we shall look in it. Maria twitches one this way, and Sophia that, and Caroline that, and Catharine t'other. We have the difficult task, all the while, of looking easy, till the approving votes are pronounced ; our only resource (which is also difficult) being to say good things to all four ; or to clap the hat upon each of their heads, and see what pretty milkwomen they make. At last the approving votes are pronounced ; and (provided it is fine) we may go forth. But how uneasy the sensation about the head ! How unlike the old hat, to which we had become used, and which must now make way for this fop of a stranger ! We might do what we liked with the former. Dust, rain, a gale of wind, a fall, a squeeze—nothing affected it. It was a true friend, a friend for all weathers. Its appearance only was against it : in everything else it was the better for wear. But if the roads or the streets are too dry, the new hat is afraid of getting dusty : if there is wind, and it is not tight, it may be blown off into the dirt : we may have to scramble after it through dust or mud, just reaching it with our fingers, only to see it blown away again. And if rain comes on ! Oh ye gallant apprentices, who have issued forth on a Sunday morning, with Jane or Susan, careless either of storms

at nightfall, or toils and scoldings next day! Ye,
who have received your new hat and boots but an hour
before ye set out; and then issue forth triumphantly,
the charmer by your side! She, with arm in yours,
and handkerchief in hand, blushing, or eating ginger-
bread, trips on: ye, admiring, trudge: we ask ye,
whether love itself has prevented ye from feeling a certain
fearful consciousness of that crowning glory, the new
and glossy hat, when the first drops of rain announce
the coming of a shower? Ah, hasten, while yet it is
of use to haste; ere yet the spotty horror fixes on the
nap! Out with the protecting handkerchief, which,
tied round the hat, and flowing off in a corner behind,
shall gleam through the thickening night like a suburb
comet! Trust not the tempting yawn of stable-yard
or gateway, or the impossible notion of a coach! The
rain will continue; and alas! ye are not so rich as in
the morning. Hasten! or think of a new hat's becoming
a rain-spout! Think of its well-built crown, its graceful
and well-measured fit, the curved-up elegance of its
rim, its shadowing gentility when seen in front, its
arching grace over the ear when beheld sideways!
Think of it also the next day! How altered, how
dejected!

> " How changed from him,
> That life of measure and that soul of rim !"

Think of the paper-like change of its consistence; of
its limp sadness—its confused and flattened nap, and
of that polished and perfect circle, which neither brush
nor hot iron shall restore!

We have here spoken of the beauties of a new hat;
but abstractedly considered, they are very problematical.
Fashion makes beauty for a time. Our ancestors found
a grace in the cocked hats now confined to beadles,
Chelsea pensioners, and coachmen. They would have

laughed at our chimney-tops with a border: though
upon the whole we do think them the more graceful
of the two. The best modern covering for the head
was the imitation of the broad Spanish hat in use about
thirty years back, when Mr. Stothard made his designs
for the *Novelist's Magazine*. But in proportion as
society has been put into a bustle, our hats seem to have
narrowed their dimensions: the flaps were clipped off
more and more till they became a rim; and now the
rim has contracted to a mere nothing; so that what
with our close heads and our tight succinct mode of
dress, we look as if we were intended for nothing but
to dart backwards and forwards on matters of business,
with as little hindrance to each other as possible.

This may give us a greater distaste to the hat than
it deserves; but good-looking or not, we know of no
situation in which a new one can be said to be useful.
We have seen how the case is during bad weather:
but if the weather is in the finest condition possible, with
neither rain nor dust, there may be a hot sunshine;
and then the hat is too narrow to shade us: no great
evil, it is true! but we must have our pique out against
the knave, and turn him to the only account in our
power:—we must write upon him. For every other
purpose we hold him as naught. The only place a new
hat can be carried into with safety is a church; for
there is plenty of room there. There also takes place
its only union of the ornamental with the useful, if so
it is to be called: we allude to the preparatory ejaculation whispered into it by the genteel worshipper,
before he turns round and makes a bow to Mr. and Mrs.
Jones and the Miss Thompsons. There is a formula
for this occasion; and doubtless it is often used, to
say nothing of extempore effusions: but there are
wicked imaginations who suspect that instead of
devouter whisperings, the communer with his lining

sometimes ejaculates no more than Swallow, St. James's Street ; or, Augarde and Spain, Hatters, No. 51 Oxford Street, London :—after which he draws up his head with infinite gravity and preparation, and makes the gentle recognitions aforesaid.

But wherever there is a crowd, the new hat is worse than useless. It is a pity that the general retrenchment of people's finances did away with the flat opera hat, which was a very sensible thing. The round one is only in the way. The matting over the floor of the Opera does not hinder it from getting dusty ; not to mention its chance of a kick from the inconsiderate. But from the pit of the other theatres you may bring it away covered with sawdust, or rubbed up all the wrong way of the nap, or monstrously squeezed into a shapeless lump. The least thing to be expected in a pressure is a great poke in its side like a sunken cheek.

Boating is a mortal enemy to new hats. A shower has you fast in a common boat ; or a sail-line, or an inexperienced oar, may knock the hat off ; and then fancy it tilting over the water with the tide, soaked all the while beyond redemption, and escaping from the tips of your outstretched fingers, while you ought all to be pulling the contrary way home.

But of all wrong boxes for a new hat, avoid a mail-coach. If you keep it on, you will begin nodding perhaps at midnight, and then it goes jamming against the side of the coach, to the equal misery of its nap and your own. If you take it off, where is its refuge ? Will the clergyman take the least heed of it, who is snoring comfortably in his nightcap ? Or will the farmer, jolting about inexorably ? Or the regular traveller, who, in his fur-cap and infinite knowledge of highway conveniences, has already beheld it with contempt ? Or the old market-woman, whom it is in vain to request to be tender ? Or the young damsel, who wonders how you can think of sleeping in such a thing ? In the morning you suddenly miss your hat, and ask after it with trepidation. The traveller smiles. They all move their legs, but know nothing of it ; till the market-woman exclaims, " Deary me ! Well— Lord, only think ! A hat is it, sir ? Why, I do believe —but I'm sure I never thought o' such a thing more than the child unborn—that it must be a hat then which I took for a pan I've been a-buying ; and so I've had my warm foot in it, Lord help us, ever since five o'clock this blessed morning ! "

It is but fair to add, that we happen to have an educated antipathy to the hat. At our school no hats were worn, and the cap is too small to be a substitute. Its only use is to astonish the old ladies in the street, who wonder how so small a thing can be kept on ; and to this end we used to rub it into the back or side of the head, where it hung like a worsted wonder. It is after the fashion of Catharine's cap in the play : it seems as if

> " Moulded on a porringer ;
> Why, 'tis a cockle, or a walnut shell,
> A knack, a toy, a trick, a baby's cap ;
> A custard coffin, a bauble."

But we may not add

> " I love thee well, in that thou likest it not ; "

Ill befall us if we ever dislike anything about thee, old nurse of our childhood ! How independent of the weather used we to feel in our old friar's dress—our thick shoes, yellow worsted stockings, and coarse long coat or gown ! Our cap was oftener in our hand than on our head, let the weather be what it would. We felt a pride as well as pleasure, when everybody else was hurrying through the streets, in receiving the full summer showers with uncovered poll, sleeking our glad hair like the feathers of a bird.

It must be said for hats in general, that they are a very ancient part of dress, perhaps the most ancient ; for a negro, who has nothing else upon him, sometimes finds it necessary to guard off the sun with a hat of leaves or straw. The Chinese, who carry their records farther back than any other people, are a hatted race, both narrow-brimmed and broad. We are apt to think of the Greeks as a bare-headed people ; and they liked to be so ; but they had hats for journeying in, such as may be seen on the statues of Mercury, who was the god of travellers. They were large and flapped, and were sometimes fastened round under the chin like a lady's bonnet. The Eastern nations generally wore turbans, and do still, with the exception of the Persians, who have exchanged them for large conical caps of felt. The Romans copied the Greeks in their dress, as in every-thing else ; but the poorer orders wore a cap like their boasted Phrygian ancestors, resembling the one which the reader may see upon the bust of Canova's Paris. The others would put their robes about their heads upon occasion—after the fashion of the hoods of the middle ages, and of the cloth head-dresses which we see in the portraits of Dante and Petrarch. Of a similar mode are the draperies on the heads of our old Plantagenet kings and of Chaucer. The velvet cap which succeeded appears to have come from Italy, as seen in the portraits of Raphael and Titian ; and it would probably have continued till the French times of Charles the Second, for our ancestors up to that period were great admirers of Italy, had not Philip the Second of Spain come over to marry our Queen Mary. The extreme heats of Spain had forced the natives upon taking to that ingenious compound of the hat and umbrella, still known by the name of the Spanish hat. We know not whether

Philip himself wore it. His father, Charles the Fifth, who was at the top of the world, is represented as delighting in a little humble-looking cap. But we conceive it was either from Philip, or some gentleman in his train, that the hat and feather succeeded among us to the cap and jewels of Henry the Eighth. The ascendancy of Spain in those times carried it into other parts of Europe. The French, not requiring so much shade from the sun, and always playing with and altering their dress, as a child does his toy, first covered the brim with feathers, then gave them a pinch in front ; then came pinches up at the side ; and at last appeared the fierce and triple-daring cocked hat. This disappeared in our childhood, or only survived among the military, the old, and the reverend, who could not willingly part with their habitual dignity. An old beau or so would also retain it, in memory of its victories when young. We remember its going away from the heads of the footguards. The heavy dragoons retained it till lately. It is now almost sunk into the mock-heroic, and confined, as we before observed, to beadles and coachmen, etc. The modern clerical beaver, agreeably to the deliberation with which our establishments depart from all custom, is a cocked hat with the front flap let down, and only a slight pinch remaining behind. This is worn also by the judges, the lawyers being of clerical extraction. Still, however, the true cocked hat lingers here and there with a solitary old gentleman ; and wherever it appears in such company, begets a certain retrospective reverence. There was a something in its connection with the high-bred drawing-room times of the seventeenth century ; in the gallant though quaint ardour of its look ; and in its being lifted up in salutations with that deliberate loftiness, the arm arching up in front and the hand slowly raising it by the front angle with finger and thumb—that could not

easily die. We remember when our steward at school,
remarkable for his inflexible air of precision and dignity,
left off his cocked hat for a round one ; there was,
undoubtedly, though we dared only half confess it to
our minds, a sort of diminished majesty about him.
His infinite self-possession began to look remotely
finite. His Crown Imperial was a little blighted. It
was like divesting a column of its capital. But the
native stateliness was there, informing the new hat. He

> " Had not yet lost
> *All* his original beaver ; nor appeared
> Less than arch-steward ruined, and the excess
> Of glory obscured."

The late Emperor Paul had conceived such a sense of
the dignity of the cocked hat, aggravated by its having
been deposed by the round one of the French republicans,
that he ordered all persons in his dominions never to
dare be seen in public with round hats, upon pain of
being knouted and sent to Siberia.

Hats being the easiest part of the European dress to be
taken off, are doffed among us out of reverence. The
Orientals, on the same account, put off their slippers
instead of turbans, which is the reason why the Jews
still keep their heads covered during worship. The
Spanish grandees have the privilege of wearing their hats
in the royal presence, probably in commemoration of
the free spirit in which the Cortes used to crown the
sovereign ; telling him (we suppose in their corporate
capacity) that they were better men than he, but chose
him of their own free will for their master. The grandees
only claim to be as good men, unless their families are
older. There is a well-known story of a picture, in
which the Virgin Mary is represented with a label
coming out of her mouth, saying to a Spanish gentleman who has politely taken off his hat, " Cousin, be

covered." But the most interesting anecdote connected with a hat belongs to the family of the De Courcys, Lord Kinsale. One of their ancestors, at an old period of our history, having overthrown a huge and insolent champion, who had challenged the whole court, was desired by the king to ask him some favour. He requested that his descendants should have the privilege of keeping their heads covered in the royal presence, and they do so to this day. The new lord, we believe, always comes to court on purpose to vindicate his right. We have heard, that on the last occasion, probably after a long interval, some of the courtiers thought it might as well have been dispensed with ; which was a foolish as well as a jealous thing, for these exceptions only prove the royal rule. The Spanish grandees originally took their privilege instead of receiving it ; but when the spirit of it had gone, their covered heads were only so many intense recognitions of the king's dignity, which it was thought such a mighty thing to resemble. A Quaker's hat is a more formidable thing than a grandee's.

J. H. Leigh Hunt (1784–1859).

The Travels of Lysicles

Lysicles, a young Athenian, fond of travelling, has just returned to us from a voyage in Thrace. A love of observation, in other words curiosity, could have been his only motive, for he never was addicted to commerce, nor disciplined in philosophy ; and indeed were he so, Thrace is hardly the country he would have chosen. I believe he is the first that ever travelled with no other intention than to see the cities and know the manners of barbarians. He represents the soil as extremely fertile in its nature, and equally well cultivated, and the inhabitants as warlike, hospitable, and courteous. All this is credible enough, and perhaps as generally known as might be expected of regions so remote and perilous. But Lysicles will appear to you to have assumed a little more than the fair privileges of a traveller, in relating that the people have so imperfect a sense of religion as to bury the dead in the temples of the Gods, and the priests are so avaricious and shameless as to claim money for the permission of this impiety. He told us further-more that he had seen a magnificent temple, built on somewhat of a Grecian model, in the interior of which there are many flat marbles fastened with iron cramps against the walls, and serving for monuments. Con-tinuing his discourse, he assured us that these monu-ments, although none are ancient, are of all forms and dimensions, as if the Thracians were resolved to waste and abolish the symmetry they had adopted ; and that they are inscribed in an obsolete language, so that the people whom they might animate and instruct, by recording brave and virtuous actions, pass them care-lessly by, breaking off now and then a nose from a conqueror, and a wing from an agathodemon.

Thrace is governed by many princes. One of them, Teres, an Odrysan, has gained great advantages in war. No doubt, this is uninteresting to you, but it is necessary to the course of my narration. Will you believe it ? yet Lysicles is both intelligent and trust-worthy . . . will you believe that, at the return of the Thracian prince to enjoy the fruits of his victory, he ordered an architect to build an arch for himself and his army to pass under, on their road into the city ? As if a road, on such an occasion, ought not rather to be widened than narrowed ! If you will not credit this of a barbarian, who is reported to be an intelligent and prudent man in other things, you will exclaim, I fear, against the exaggeration of Lysicles and my credulity, when I relate to you on his authority that, to the same conqueror, by his command, there has been erected a column sixty cubits high, supporting his effigy in marble !

Imagine the general of an army standing upon a column of sixty cubits to show himself ! A crane might do it after a victory over a pigmy ; or it might aptly represent the virtues of a rope-dancer, exhibiting how little he was subject to dizziness.

I will write no more about it, for really I am beginning to think that some pretty Thracian has given poor Lysicles a love-potion, and that it has affected his brain.

Walter Savage Landor (1775–1864).

From " Pericles and Aspasia."

An Adventure in the South Sea Islands

It was on the first of February that we went on shore for the purpose of visiting the village. Although, as said before, we entertained not the slightest suspicion, still no proper precaution was neglected. Six men were left in the schooner, with instructions to permit none of the savages to approach the vessel during our absence, under any pretence whatever, and to remain constantly on deck. The boarding-nettings were up, the guns double-shotted with grape and canister, and the swivels loaded with canisters of musket-balls. She lay, with her anchor apeak, about a mile from the shore, and no canoe could approach her in any direction without being distinctly seen and exposed to the full fire of our swivels immediately.

The six men being left on board, our shore-party consisted of thirty-two persons in all. We were armed to the teeth, having with us muskets, pistols, and cut-

lasses, besides each a long kind of seaman's knife, somewhat resembling the Bowie-knife now so much used
throughout our western and southern country. A hundred of the black skin warriors met us at the landing
for the purpose of accompanying us on our way. We
noticed, however, with some surprise, that they were
now entirely without arms; and upon questioning Too-
wit in relation to this circumstance, he merely answered
that *Mattee non we pa pa si*—meaning that there was
no need of arms where all were brothers. We took
this in good part, and proceeded.

We had passed the spring and rivulet of which I
before spoke, and were now entering upon a narrow
gorge leading through the chain of soapstone hills among
which the village was situated. This gorge was very
rocky and uneven, so much so that it was with no little
difficulty we scrambled through it on our first visit to
Klock-Klock. The whole length of the ravine might
have been a mile and a half, or probably two miles.
It wound in every possible direction through the hills
(having apparently formed, at some remote period, the
bed of a torrent), in no instance proceeding more than
twenty yards without an abrupt turn. The sides of
this dell would have averaged, I am sure, seventy or
eighty feet in perpendicular altitude throughout the
whole of their extent, and in some portions they arose
to an astonishing height, overshadowing the pass so
completely that but little of the light of day could
penetrate. The general width was about forty feet,
and occasionally it diminished so as not to allow the
passage of more than five or six persons abreast. In
short, there could be no place in the world better adapted
for the consummation of an ambuscade, and it was no
more than natural that we should look carefully to our
arms as we entered upon it. When I now think of our
egregious folly, the chief subject of astonishment seems

to be that we should have ever ventured, under any circumstances, so completely into the power of unknown savages as to permit them to march both before and behind us in our progress through this ravine. Yet such was the order we blindly took up, trusting foolishly to the force of our party, the unarmed condition of Too-wit and his men, the certain efficacy of our fire-arms (whose effect was yet a secret to the natives), and more than all to the long-sustained pretension of friend-ship kept up by these infamous wretches. Five or six of them went on before, as if to lead the way, ostenta-tiously busying themselves in removing the larger stones and rubbish from the path. Next came our own party. We walked closely together, taking care only to prevent separation. Behind followed the main body of the savages, observing unusual order and decorum.

Dirk Peters, a man named Wilson Allen, and myself, were on the right of our companions, examining, as we went along, the singular stratification of the precipice which overhung us. A fissure in the soft rock attracted our attention. It was about wide enough for one per-son to enter without squeezing, and extended back into the hill some eighteen or twenty feet in a straight course, sloping afterwards to the left. The height of the open-ing, as far as we could see into it from the main gorge, was perhaps sixty or seventy feet. There were one or two stunted shrubs growing from the crevices, bearing a species of filbert, which I felt some curiosity to examine, and pushed in briskly for that purpose, gathering five or six of the nuts at a grasp, and then hastily retreating. As I turned, I found that Peters and Allen had followed me. I desired them to go back, as there was not room for two persons to pass, saying they should have some of my nuts. They accordingly turned, and were scram-bling back, Allen being close to the mouth of the fissure, when I was suddenly aware of a concussion resembling nothing I had ever before experienced, and which impressed me with a vague conception, if indeed I then thought of anything, that the whole foundations of the solid globe were suddenly rent asunder, and that the day of universal dissolution was at hand.

* * *

As soon as I could collect my scattered senses, I found myself nearly suffocated, and grovelling in utter darkness among a quantity of loose earth, which was also falling upon me heavily in every direction, threatening to bury me entirely. Horribly alarmed at this idea, I struggled to gain my feet, and at length succeeded. I then remained motionless for some moments, endeavouring to conceive what had happened to me, and where I was. Presently I heard a deep groan just at my ear, and afterwards the smothered voice of Peters calling to me for aid in the name of God. I scrambled one or two paces forward, when I fell directly over the head and shoulders of my companion, who, I soon discovered, was buried in a loose mass of earth as far as his middle, and struggling desperately to free himself from the pressure. I tore the dirt from around him with all the energy I could command, and at length succeeded in getting him out.

As soon as we sufficiently recovered from our fright and surprise to be capable of conversing rationally, we both came to the conclusion that the walls of the fissure in which we had ventured had, by some convulsion of nature, or probably from their own weight, caved in overhead, and that we were consequently lost for ever, being thus entombed alive. For a long time we gave up supinely to the most intense agony and despair, such as cannot be adequately imagined by those who have never been in a similar situation. I firmly believed

H

that no incident ever occurring in the course of human events is more adapted to inspire the supremeness of mental and bodily distress than a case like our own, of living inhumation. The blackness of darkness which envelops the victim, the terrific oppression of lungs, the stifling fumes from the damp earth, unite with the ghastly considerations that we are beyond the remotest confines of hope, and that such is the allotted portion of *the dead*, to carry into the human heart a degree of appalling awe and horror not to be tolerated—never to be conceived.

At length Peters proposed that we should endeavour to ascertain precisely the extent of our calamity, and grope about our prison ; it being barely possible, he observed, that some opening might be yet left us for escape. I caught eagerly at this hope, and arousing myself to exertion, attempted to force my way through the loose earth. Hardly had I advanced a single step before a glimmer of light became perceptible, enough to convince me that, at all events, we should not immediately perish for want of air. We now took some degree of heart, and encouraged each other to hope for the best. Having scrambled over a bank of rubbish which impeded our farther progress in the direction of the light, we found less difficulty in advancing, and also experienced some relief from the excessive oppression of lungs which had tormented us. Presently we were enabled to obtain a glimpse of the objects around, and discovered that we were near the extremity of the straight portion of the fissure, where it made a turn to the left. A few struggles more, and we reached the bend, when, to our inexpressible joy, there appeared a long seam or crack extending upward a vast distance, generally at an angle of about forty-five degrees, although sometimes much more precipitous. We could not see through the whole extent of this opening ; but as a good deal

of light came down it, we had little doubt of finding
at the top of it (if we could by any means reach the
top) a clear passage into the open air.

I now called to mind that three of us had entered the
fissure from the main gorge, and that our companion,
Allen, was still missing; we determined at once to
retrace our steps and look for him. After a long search,
and much danger from the farther caving in of the
earth above us, Peters at length cried out to me that
he had hold of our companion's foot, and that his whole
body was deeply buried beneath the rubbish, beyond a
possibility of extricating him. I soon found that what
he said was too true, and that, of course, life had been
long extinct. With sorrowful hearts, therefore, we left
the corpse to its fate, and again made our way to the
bend.

The breadth of the seam was barely sufficient to
admit us, and after one or two ineffectual efforts at
getting up, we began once more to despair. I have
before said that the chain of hills through which ran
the main gorge was composed of a species of soft rock
resembling soap-stone. The sides of the cleft we were
now attempting to ascend were of the same material,
and so excessively slippery, being wet, that we could
get but little foothold upon them, even in their least
precipitous parts; in some places, where the ascent
was nearly perpendicular, the difficulty was of course
much aggravated; and indeed for some time, we thought
it insurmountable. We took courage, however from
despair; and what, by dint of cutting steps in the soft
stone with our Bowie-knives, and swinging, at the risk
of our lives, to small projecting points of a harder species
of slaty rock which now and then protruded from the
general mass, we at length reached a natural platform,
from which was perceptible a patch of blue sky, at the
extremity of a thickly-wooded ravine. Looking back

now, with somewhat more leisure, at the passage through which we had thus far proceeded, we clearly saw, from the appearance of its sides, that it was of late formation, and we concluded that the concussion, whatever it was, which had so unexpectedly overwhelmed us, had also at the same moment laid open this path for escape. Being quite exhausted with exertion, and indeed so weak that we were scarcely able to stand or articulate, Peters now proposed that we should endeavour to bring our companions to the rescue by firing the pistols which still remained in our girdles—the muskets as well as cutlasses had been lost among the loose earth at the bottom of the chasm. Subsequent events proved that, had we fired, we should have sorely repented it ; but luckily a half suspicion of foul play had by this time arisen in my mind, and we forbore to let the savages know of our whereabouts.

After having reposed for about an hour we pushed on slowly up the ravine, and had gone no great way before we heard a succession of tremendous yells. At length we reached what might be called the surface of the ground, for our path hitherto, since leaving the platform, had lain beneath an archway of high rock and foliage, at a vast distance overhead. With great caution we stole to a narrow opening through which we had a clear sight of the surrounding country, when the whole dreadful secret of the concussion broke upon us in one moment and at one view.

The spot from which we looked was not far from the summit of the highest peak in the range of the soap-stone hills. The gorge in which our party of thirty-two had entered ran within fifty feet to the left of us. But for at least one hundred yards the channel or bed of this gorge was entirely filled up with the chaotic ruins of more than a million tons of earth and stone that had been artificially tumbled within it. The means

by which the vast mass had been precipitated were not
more simple than evident, for sure traces of the mur-
derous work were yet remaining. In several spots along
the top of the eastern side of the gorge (we were now on
the western) might be seen stakes of wood driven into
the earth. In these spots the earth had not given way,
but throughout the whole extent of the face of the
precipice from which the mass *had* fallen, it was clear,
from marks left in the soil resembling those made by
the drill of the rock-blaster, that stakes similar to those
we saw standing had been inserted at not more than a
yard apart, for the length of perhaps three hundred
feet, and ranging at about ten feet back from the edge
of the gulf. Strong cords of grape-vine were attached
to the stakes still remaining on the hill, and it was
evident that such cords had also been attached to each
of the other stakes. I have already spoken of the
singular stratification of these soapstone hills, and the
description just given of the narrow and deep fissure
through which we effected our escape from inhumation
will afford a further conception of its nature. This
was such that almost every natural convulsion would
be sure to split the soil into perpendicular layers or
ridges running parallel with one another, and a very
moderate exertion of art would be sufficient for effect-
ing the same purpose. Of this stratification the savages
had availed themselves to accomplish their treacherous
ends. There can be no doubt that by the continuous
line of stakes a partial rupture of the soil had been
brought about, probably to the depth of one or two
feet, when by means of a savage pulling at the end of
each of the cords (these cords being attached to the
tops of the stakes and extending back from the edge of
the cliff) a vast leverage power was obtained, capable
of hurling the whole face of the hill upon a given signal
into the bosom of the abyss below. The fate of our

poor companions was no longer a matter of uncertainty. We alone had escaped from the tempest of that over-whelming destruction. We were the only living white men upon the island.

Edgar Allan Poe (1809–1849).

From " The Narrative of Arthur Gordon Pym."

De Quincey on Shakespeare

It becomes our duty to take a summary survey of his works, of his intellectual powers, and of his station in literature,—a station which is now irrevocably settled, not so much (which happens in other cases) by a vast overbalance of favourable suffrages, as by acclamation ; not so much by the *voices* of those who admire him up to the verge of idolatry, as by the *acts* of those who everywhere seek for his works among the primal neces-sities of life, demand them, and crave them as they do their daily bread ; not so much by eulogy openly pro-claiming itself, as by the silent homage recorded in the endless multiplication of what he has bequeathed us ; not so much by his own compatriots, who, with regard to almost every other author, compose the total amount of his *effective* audience, as by the unanimous " All hail ! " of intellectual Christendom ; finally, not by the hasty partisanship of his own generation, nor by the biassed judgment of an age trained in the same modes of feeling and of thinking with himself, but by the solemn award of generation succeeding to generation, of one age correcting the obliquities or peculiarities of another ; by the verdict of [many] years . . . ; a verdict which has been continually revived and re-opened, probed, searched, vexed, by criticism in every spirit, from the most genial and intelligent, down to the most malignant and scur-

rilously hostile which feeble heads and great ignorance
could suggest when co-operating with impure hearts
and narrow sensibilities ; a verdict, in short, sustained
and countersigned by a longer series of writers, many
of them eminent for wit or learning, than were ever
before congregated upon any inquest relating to any
author, be he who he might, ancient or modern, Pagan
or Christian. It was a most witty saying with respect
to a piratical and knavish publisher, who made a trade
of insulting the memories of deceased authors by forged
writings, that he was " among the new terrors of death."
But in the gravest sense it may be affirmed of Shakespeare that he is among the modern luxuries of life ;
that life, in fact, is a new thing, and one more to be
coveted, since Shakespeare has extended the domains
of human consciousness, and pushed its dark frontiers
into regions not so much as dimly descried or even sus-
pected before his time, far less illuminated (as now they
are) by beauty and tropical luxuriance of life.

Thomas de Quincey (1785–1859).

From his article on " Shakespeare " contributed to
the 7th edition of the " Encyclopædia Britannica," 1838.

A Swim in the Rapids of Niagara

Monday 5th August [1833], Eagle Hotel, Niagara.

To-day I have been mortified, bitterly. The morning
was hot and cloudless, I sauntered along the brink of
the Rapids, descended the long tiresome spiral stair-
case which leads directly to the ferry on the river.

Instead of crossing over in the boat to Canada, I
threaded my way along the rugged and rocky shore.
I came to a solitary hollow by the river side, about a
mile below the Falls. The agitated water mining the

banks, had broadened its bed and covered the shelving shore there with massy fragments of dark limestone rocks. The mural cliffs rose on each side two or three hundred feet almost perpendicularly, yet pine trees and cypress and yew managed to scale the steep ascent and to hold their ground, boring into the hard rocks with their harder roots, till, undermined by the continual rising of the water, they had fallen. Even at this distance from the Falls the waters in the mid-channel were still boiling and bubbling and covered with foam, raging along and spreading out in all directions. Pieces of timber I threw in spun round in concentric circles. Then turning and twisting against the rocks like crushed serpents, it flowed on to the Rapids and formed dangerous whirlpools two miles lower down. Above the Falls this river is a mile broad, where I was now it was less than half a mile, above and below me not more than a quarter ; so that flowing through a deep ravine of rocks it was very deep even to its brink, and in the centre they say above a hundred feet. The sun was now at its zenith and its rays concentrated into the tunnel made my brains boil, the water was not agitated, was of that tempting emerald green which looks so voluptuously cool like molten jasper flaked with snow.

I never resist the syren pleasure, when she is surrounded by her water nymphs in their sea green mantles, and my blood is boiling. I hastily cast aside my clothes, with nerves throbbing and panting breast, and clambering up to a ledge of rock jutting over a clear deep pool, I spring in head foremost. In an instant every nerve was restrung and set to the tune of vigorous boyhood. I spring up and gambol between wind and water.

To excel in swimming long and strong limbs and a pliant body are indispensable, the chest too should be broad, the greatest breadth of most fish is close to the head ; the back must be bent inwards (incavated), the

head reined back like a swan's and the chest thrown
forward ; thus the body will float without exertion.
The legs and arms after striking out should be drawn
up and pressed close together, and five seconds between
each stroke, as in running distances so in swimming
distances, it is indispensable. Your life depends upon
it, avoid being blown, the strongest swimmer, like the
strongest horse, is done when his respiration fails.
Utterly regardless of these truths, notwithstanding it
is the pure gold of personal experience, in the wanton
pride of my strength and knowledge of the art, I gam-
bolled and played all sorts of gymnastics ; methought
the water, all wild as it was, was too sluggish, so I
wheeled into mid-channel and dashing down the stream
I was determined to try my strength in those places
where the waters are wildest. I floated for some time
over the eddying whirls without much difficulty and
then struck through them right across the river.

This triumph steeled my confidence of " the ice
brook's temper," after gaining breath regardless that
I had changed the field of action in having been borne
a long way down the river, consequently that I was
rapidly approaching the Rapids, which nor boat nor
anything with life can live in.

Well, thinking alone of the grandeur and wildness of
the scene I swam on without difficulty, yet I felt the
chill that follows over-exertion stealing up my extremities, cramping my toes and fingers with sudden twitches.
I was again returned to the centre of the vortical part
of the river, I was out of sight of the Falls, the water
was becoming rougher and rougher, I was tossed about
and drifting fast down. I now remembered the terrible
whirlpool below me, I could make no progress, the stream
was mastering me. I thought I had no time to lose
so I incautiously put forth my strength, springing in
the water with energy to cross the arrowy stream trans-

versely, conceiving that when I reached the smoother
part, out of the vortex of mid-channel, my work was
done. I seemed to be held by the legs and sucked
downwards, the scumming surf broke over and blinded
me, I began to ship water. In the part of the river I
had now drifted to the water was frightfully agitated,
it was broken and raging all around me ; still my exertions augmented with the opposition, I breathed quicker
and with increasing difficulty, I kept my eye steadily
on the dark-browed precipice before me, it seemed receding, I thought of returning, but the distance and difficulty was equally balanced ; the rotary action of the
water under its surface, when I relaxed my exertions,
sucked my body, heels foremost, downwards. Whilst
breathing hard I swallowed the spray, my strength
suddenly declined, I was compelled to keep my mouth
open panting and gasping, my lower extremities sank.
I looked around to see if there was any timber floating,
or any boat or person on the shore. There was nothing, and if there had been no one could have seen me
enveloped in spray, and the distant voice of the Falls
drowned all other sounds : the thought that my time
was come at last flashed across my mind, I thought
what a fool I was to blindly abuse my own gained knowledge and thus cast myself away ; the lessons of experience like the inscriptions on tombs grow faint and
illegible if not continually renewed. Why did I attempt
to cross a part of the river that none had ever crossed
before ? There was not even the excitement of a fool
on the shore to see or say he had seen me do it. Why
had I not spoken to the man at the ferry, he would
have followed me in his boat. I remembered too hearing the thing was not practicable ; why what a way-
ward fool am I. These things acted as a spur, these
truths crossed my mind rapidly, and I thought of all
the scenes of drowning I had seen ; of my own repeated

perils that way. I heard the voices of the dead calling
to me, I actually thought, as my mind grew darker,
that they were tugging at my feet. Aston's horrid
death by drowning nearly paralysed me. I endeavoured
in vain to shake off these thick-coming fancies, they
glowed before me. Thus I lay suspended between life
and death. I was borne fearfully and rapidly along, I
had lost all power, I could barely keep my head above
the surface, I waxed fainter and fainter, there was no
possibility of help. I occasionally turned on my back
to rest and endeavour to recover my breath, but the
agitation of the water and surf got into my mouth and
nostrils, the water stuck in my throat, which was instantly followed by the agonizing sensation of strangu-
lation. This I well knew was an unerring first symptom
of a suffocating death. Instead of air I sucked in the
flying spray it's impossible either to swallow or cast
out again, and whilst struggling to do either I only
drew in more. The torture of choking was terrible,
my limbs were cold and almost lifeless, my stomach
too was cramped. I saw the waters of the Rapids
below me raging and all about hissing. I thought now
how much I would have given for a spiked nail so fixed
that I could have rested the ball of my toe on it for
one instant and have drawn one gulp of air unimpeded,
to have swallowed the water that was sticking in the
mid-channel of my windpipe; nay I would have been
glad at any risk to have rested on the point of a lancet.
I had settled down till I was suspended in the water,
the throbbing and heaving of my breast and heart and
increased swelling in my throat had now so completely
paralysed my limbs, that [I thought ?] of giving up a
struggle which seemed hopeless. My uppermost thought
was mortification at this infallible proof of my declin-
ing strength, well I knew there was a time in which I
could have forced my way through ten times these

impediments ; the only palliation I could think of was
the depth and icy chilliness of the water which came
straight from the regions of the frigid zone. This contracted all my muscles and sinews, my head grew dizzy
from bending the spine backwards, the blow I had
received from the upset I had not recovered ; the ball,
too, immediately over my jugular vein retards the cir-
culation ; my right arm has never recovered its strength
and it was now benumbed. All this and much more I
thought of, my body said I " is like a leaky skiff " no
longer sea-worthy, and " my soul shall swim out of it "
and free myself. I thought the links which held me
to life were so worn that the shock which broke them
would be slight. It had always been my prayer to die
in the pride of my strength,—age, however it approached,
with wealth and power, or on crutches and in rags, was
to me equally loathsome,—better to perish before he
had touched [me] with his withering finger, in this wild
place, on a foreign shore. Niagara " chanting a thunder
psalm " as a requiem was a fitting end to my wild
meteor-like life. Thoughts like these absorbed me. I
no longer in the bitterness of my heart struggled against
the waters which whirled me along, and certainly this
despair as if in mockery preserved me. For looking
again towards the shore I saw that I had been carried
nearer to it, and without any exertion on my part I
floated lighter, the under-tow no longer drew me down,
and presently the water became smooth, I had been cast
out of the vortex and was drifting towards the rocks.
I heard the boiling commotion of the tremendous Rapids
and saw the spume flying in the air a little below me,
and then I lay stranded, sick and dizzy, everything still
seemed whirling round and round and the waters singing in my ears. The sun had descended behind the
cliffs, and my limbs shook so violently that I could not
stand ; I lay there for some time, and then, as the rocks

were too rugged to admit of walking, I swam slowly up along the shore. I was deeply mortified, the maxim which has so long borne me towards my desires triumphantly—go on till you are stopped—fails me here. I have been stopped, there is no denying it, death would have pained me less than this conviction. I must change my vaunting crest.

My shadow trembling on the black rock as reflected by the last rays of the setting sun, shows me as in a glass, that my youth and strength have fled. When I had recovered my breath I dressed myself and walked sullenly to the ferry boat. I took the two heavy oars and exerting my utmost strength bent them like rattans as I forced the clumsy boat against the stream. The ferry man where I landed seemed surprised at my impetuosity, he said the sun's been so hot to-day that he was dead beat, I said, " Why how old are you ? " " Oh," he said, " that's nothing "—he was thirty-eight. " Thirty-eight," I echoed, " then you are not worth a damn, you had better look out for the almshouse." I started off running up the steep acclivity and heard him muttering " Why, you aren't so very young yourself ; what the devil does he mean ? " When I got to the summit I threw myself down on a ledge of rock, instead of over as I should have done, and fell asleep, and thus ended the day ; I shall not however forget it.

Edward John Trelawny (1792–1881).

From " Letters of Edward John Trelawny," edited by Buxton Forman, by permission of Mr. Humphry Milford.

Squeers

Mr. Squeers' appearance was not prepossessing. He had but one eye, and the popular prejudice runs in favour of two. The eye he had was unquestionably useful, but decidedly not ornamental : being of a greenish grey, and in shape resembling the fan-light of a street door. The blank side of his face was much wrinkled and puckered up, which gave him a very sinister appearance, especially when he smiled, at which times his expression bordered closely on the villainous. His hair was very flat and shiny, save at the ends, where it was brushed stiffly up from a low protruding forehead, which assorted well with his harsh voice and coarse manner. He was about two or three and fifty, and a trifle below the middle size ; he wore a white neckerchief with long ends, and a suit of scholastic black ; but his coat sleeves being a great deal too long, and his trousers a great deal too short, he appeared ill at ease in his clothes, and as if he were in a perpetual state of astonishment at finding himself so respectable.

Mr. Squeers was standing in a box by one of the coffee-room fire-places, fitted with one such table as is usually seen in coffee-rooms, and two of extraordinary shapes and dimensions made to suit the angles of the partition. In a corner of the seat was a very small deal trunk, tied round with a scanty piece of cord ; and on the trunk was perched—his lace-up half-boots and corduroy trousers dangling in the air—a diminutive boy, with his shoulders drawn up to his ears, and his hands planted on his knees, who glanced timidly at the schoolmaster from time to time, with evident dread and apprehension.

" Half-past three," muttered Mr. Squeers, turning from the window, and looking sulkily at the coffee-room clock. " There will be nobody here to-day."

Much vexed by this reflection, Mr. Squeers looked at the little boy to see whether he was doing anything he could beat him for. As he happened not to be doing anything at all, he merely boxed his ears, and told him not to do it again.

"At Midsummer," muttered Mr. Squeers, resuming his complaint, "I took down ten boys ; ten twentys is two hundred pound. I go back at eight o'clock to-morrow morning, and have got only three—three oughts is an ought—three twos is six—sixty pound. What's come of all the boys ? what's parents got in their heads ? what does it all mean ? "

Here the little boy on the top of the trunk gave a violent sneeze.

"Halloa, sir ! " growled the schoolmaster, turning round. "What's that, sir ? "

"Nothing, please sir," said the little boy.

"Nothing, sir ! " exclaimed Mr. Squeers.

"Please sir, I sneezed," rejoined the boy, trembling till the little trunk shook under him.

"Oh ! sneezed, did you ? " retorted Mr. Squeers. "Then what did you say ' nothing ' for, sir ? "

In default of a better answer to this question, the little boy screwed a couple of knuckles into each of his eyes and began to cry, wherefore Mr. Squeers knocked him off the trunk with a blow on one side of his face, and knocked him on again with a blow on the other.

"Wait till I get you down into Yorkshire, my young gentleman," said Mr. Squeers, "and then I'll give you the rest. Will you hold that noise, sir ? "

"Ye—ye—yes," sobbed the little boy, rubbing his face very hard with the Beggar's Petition in printed calico.

"Then do so at once, sir," said Squeers. "Do you hear ? "

As this admonition was accompanied with a threatening gesture, and uttered with a savage aspect, the little boy rubbed his face harder, as if to keep the tears back ;

and, beyond alternately sniffing and choking, gave no further vent to his emotions.

"Mr. Squeers," said the waiter, looking in at this juncture; "here's a gentleman asking for you at the bar."

"Show the gentleman in, Richard," replied Mr. Squeers, in a soft voice. "Put your handkerchief in your pocket, you little scoundrel, or I'll murder you when the gentleman goes."

The schoolmaster had scarcely uttered these words in a fierce whisper, when the stranger entered. Affecting not to see him, Mr. Squeers feigned to be intent upon mending a pen, and offering benevolent advice to his youthful pupil.

"My dear child," said Mr. Squeers, "all people have their trials. This early trial of yours that is fit to make your little heart burst, and your very eyes come out of your head with crying, what is it ? Nothing ; less than nothing. You are leaving your friends, but you will have a father in me, my dear, and a mother in Mrs. Squeers. At the delightful village of Dotheboys, near Greta Bridge in Yorkshire, where youth are boarded, clothed, booked, washed, furnished with pocket-money, provided with all necessaries——"

"It *is* the gentleman," observed the stranger, stopping the schoolmaster in the rehearsal of his advertisement. "Mr. Squeers, I believe, sir ? "

"The same, sir," said Mr. Squeers, with an assumption of extreme surprise.

"The gentleman," said the stranger, "that advertised in the *Times* newspaper ? "

"—*Morning Post, Chronicle, Herald,* and *Advertiser,* regarding the Academy called Dotheboys Hall at the delightful village of Dotheboys, near Greta Bridge in Yorkshire," added Mr. Squeers. "You come on business, sir. I see by my young friends. How do you

do, my little gentleman ? and how do *you* do, sir ? "
With this salutation Mr. Squeers patted the heads of
two hollow-eyed, small-boned little boys, whom the
applicant had brought with him, and waited for further
communications.

" I am in the oil and colour way. My name is Snawley, sir," said the stranger.

Squeers inclined his head as much as to say, " And a
remarkably pretty name, too."

The stranger continued. " I have been thinking,
Mr. Squeers, of placing my two boys at your school."

" It is not for me to say so, sir," replied Mr. Squeers,
" but I don't think you could possibly do a better thing."

" Hem ! " said the other. " Twenty pounds per
annewum, I believe, Mr. Squeers ? "

" Guineas," rejoined the schoolmaster, with a per-
suasive smile.

" Pounds for two, I think, Mr. Squeers," said Mr.
Snawley solemnly.

" I don't think it could be done, sir," replied Squeers,
as if he had never considered the proposition before.
" Let me see ; four fives is twenty, double that, and
deduct the—well, a pound either way shall not stand
betwixt us. You must recommend me to your connection, sir, and make it up that way."

" They are not great eaters," said Mr. Snawley.

" Oh ! that doesn't matter at all," replied Squeers.
" We don't consider the boys' appetites at our establishment." This was strictly true ; they did not.

" Every wholesome luxury, sir, that Yorkshire can
afford," continued Squeers ; " every beautiful moral
that Mrs. Squeers can instil ; every—in short, every
comfort of a home that a boy could wish for, will be
theirs, Mr. Snawley."

" I should wish their morals to be particularly attended
to," said Mr. Snawley.

" I am glad of that, sir," replied the schoolmaster, drawing himself up. " They have come to the right shop for morals, sir."

" You are a moral man yourself," said Mr. Snawley.

" I rather believe I am, sir," replied Squeers.

" I have the satisfaction to know you are, sir," said Mr. Snawley. " I asked one of your references, and he said you were pious."

" Well, sir, I hope I am a little in that line," replied Squeers.

" I hope I am also," rejoined the other. " Could I say a few words with you in the next box ? "

" By all means," rejoined Squeers with a grin. " My dears, will you speak to your new playfellow a minute or two ? That is one of my boys, sir. Belling his name is,—a Taunton boy that, sir."

" Is he, indeed ? " rejoined Mr. Snawley, looking at the poor little urchin as if he were some extraordinary natural curiosity.

" He goes down with me to-morrow, sir," said Squeers. " That's his luggage that he is a sitting upon now. Each boy is required to bring, sir, two suits of clothes, six shirts, six pair of stockings, two nightcaps, two pocket-handkerchiefs, two pair of shoes, two hats, and a razor."

" A razor ! " exclaimed Mr. Snawley, as they walked into the next box. " What for ? "

" To shave with," replied Squeers, in a slow and measured tone.

There was not much in these three words, but there must have been something in the manner in which they were said, to attract attention ; for the schoolmaster and his companion looked steadily at each other for a few seconds, and then exchanged a very meaning smile. Snawley was a sleek, flat-nosed man, clad in sombre garments, and long black gaiters, and bearing in his countenance an expression of much mortification and sanctity; so, his smiling without any obvious reason was the more remarkable.

" Up to what age do you keep boys at your school then ? " he asked at length.

" Just as long as their friends make the quarterly payments to my agent in town, or until such time as they run away," replied Squeers. " Let us understand each other ; I see we may safely do so. What are these boys ;—natural children ? "

" No," rejoined Snawley, meeting the gaze of the schoolmaster's one eye. " They ain't."

" I thought they might be," said Squeers, coolly. " We have a good many of them ; that boy's one."

" Him in the next box ? " said Snawley.

Squeers nodded in the affirmative ; his companion took another peep at the little boy on the trunk, and turning round again, looked as if he were quite disappointed to see him so much like other boys, and said he should hardly have thought it.

" He is," cried Squeers. " But about these boys of yours ; you wanted to speak to me ? "

" Yes," replied Snawley. " The fact is, I am not their father, Mr. Squeers. I'm only their step-father."

" Oh ! Is that it ? " said the schoolmaster. " That explains it at once. I was wondering what the devil you were going to send them to Yorkshire for. Ha ! ha ! Oh, I understand now."

" You see I have married the mother," pursued Snawley ; " it's expensive keeping boys at home, and as she has a little money in her own right, I am afraid (women are so very foolish, Mr. Squeers) that she might be led to squander it on them, which would be their ruin, you know."

" *I* see," returned Squeers, throwing himself back in his chair, and waving his hand.

" And this," resumed Snawley, " has made me anxious

to put them to some school a good distance off, where
there are no holidays—none of those ill-judged comings
home twice a year that unsettle children's minds so—
and where they may rought it a little—you compre-
hend ? "

" The payments regular, and no questions asked,"
said Squeers, nodding his head.

" That's it, exactly," rejoined the other. " Morals
strictly attended to, though."

" Strictly," said Squeers.

" Not too much writing home allowed, I suppose ? "
said the step-father, hesitating.

" None, except a circular at Christmas, to say they
never were so happy, and hope they may never be sent
for," rejoined Squeers.

" Nothing could be better," said the step-father, rubbing his hands.

" Then, as we understand each other," said Squeers,
" will you allow me to ask you whether you consider
me a highly virtuous, exemplary, and well-conducted
man in private life ; and whether, as a person whose
business it is to take charge of youth, you place the
strongest confidence in my unimpeachable integrity,
liberality, religious principles, and ability ? "

" Certainly I do," replied the step-father, reciprocat-
ing the schoolmaster's grin.

" Perhaps you won't object to say that, if I make
you a reference ? "

" Not the least in the world."

" That's your sort ! " said Squeers, taking up a pen ;
" this is doing business, and that's what I like."

Having entered Mr. Snawley's address, the schoolmaster had next to perform the still more agreeable
office of entering the receipt of the first quarter's payment in advance, which he had scarcely completed,
when another voice was heard inquiring for Mr. Squeers.

" Here he is," replied the schoolmaster ; " what is it ? "

" Only a matter of business, sir," said Ralph Nickleby, presenting himself, closely followed by Nicholas. " There was an advertisement of yours in the papers this morning ? "

" There was, sir. This way, if you please," said Squeers, who had by this time got back to the box by the fire-place. " Won't you be seated ? "

" Why, I think I will," replied Ralph, suiting the action to the word, and placing his hat on the table before him. " This is my nephew, sir, Mr. Nicholas Nickleby."

" How do you do, sir ? " said Squeers.

Nicholas bowed, said he was very well, and seemed very much astonished at the outward appearance of the proprietor of Dotheboys Hall : as indeed he was.

" Perhaps you recollect me ? " said Ralph, looking narrowly at the schoolmaster.

" You paid me a small account at each of my half-yearly visits to town, for some years, I think, sir," replied Squeers.

" I did," rejoined Ralph.

" For the parents of a boy named Dorker, who unfortunately——"

" —unfortunately died at Dotheboys Hall," said Ralph, finishing the sentence.

" I remember very well, sir," rejoined Squeers. " Ah ! Mrs. Squeers, sir, was as partial to that lad as if he had been her own ; the attention, sir, that was bestowed upon that boy in his illness ! Dry toast and warm tea offered him every night and morning when he couldn't swallow anything—a candle in his bedroom on the very night he died—the best dictionary sent up for him to lay his head upon—I don't regret it though. It is a pleasant thing to reflect that one did one's duty by him."

Ralph smiled, as if he meant anything but smiling, and looked round at the strangers present.

"These are only some pupils of mine," said Wackford Squeers, pointing to the little boy on the trunk and the two little boys on the floor, who had been staring at each other without uttering a word, and writhing their bodies into most remarkable contortions, according to the custom of little boys when they first become acquainted. "This gentleman, sir, is a parent who is kind enough to compliment me upon the course of education adopted at Dotheboys Hall, which is situated, sir, at the delightful village of Dotheboys, near Greta Bridge in Yorkshire, where youth are boarded, clothed, booked, washed, furnished with pocket-money——"

"Yes, we know all about that, sir," interrupted Ralph, testily. "It's in the advertisement."

"You are very right, sir ; it *is* in the advertisement," replied Squeers.

"And in the matter of fact besides," interrupted Mr. Snawley. "I feel bound to assure you, sir, and I am proud to have this opportunity *of* assuring you, that I consider Mr. Squeers a gentleman highly virtuous, exemplary, well-conducted, and——"

"I make no doubt of it, sir," interrupted Ralph, checking the torrent of recommendation ; "no doubt of it at all. Suppose we come to business ? "

"With all my heart, sir," rejoined Squeers. " 'Never postpone business,' is the very first lesson we instil into our commercial pupils. Master Belling, my dear, always remember that ; do you hear ? "

"Yes, sir," repeated Master Belling.

"He recollects what it is, does he ? " said Ralph.

"Tell the gentleman," said Squeers.

"Never," repeated Master Belling.

"Very good," said Squeers ; "go on."

" Never," repeated Master Belling again.

" Very good indeed," said Squeers. " Yes."

" P," suggested Nicholas good-naturedly.

" Perform—business ! " said Master Belling. " Never
—perform—business ! "

" Very well, sir," said Squeers, darting a withering
look at the culprit. " You and I will perform a little
business on our private account by and bye."

" And just now," said Ralph, " we had better transact
our own, perhaps."

" If you please," said Squeers.

" Well," resumed Ralph, " it's brief enough ; soon
broached ; and I hope easily concluded. You have
advertised for an able assistant, sir ? "

" Precisely so," said Squeers.

" And you really want one ? "

" Certainly," answered Squeers.

" Here he is ! " said Ralph. " My nephew Nicholas,
hot from school, with everything he learnt there fermenting in his head, and nothing fermenting in his
pocket, is just the man you want."

" I am afraid," said Squeers, perplexed with such an
application from a youth of Nicholas's figure, " I am
afraid the young man won't suit me."

" Yes, he will," said Ralph ; " I know better. Don't
be cast down, sir ; you will be teaching all the young
noblemen in Dotheboys Hall in less than a week's time,
unless this gentleman is more obstinate than I take
him to be."

" I fear, sir," said Nicholas, addressing Mr. Squeers,
" that you object to my youth, and to my not being a
Master of Arts ? "

" The absence of a college degree *is* an objection,"
replied Squeers, looking as grave as he could, and considerably puzzled, no less by the contrast between the
simplicity of the nephew and the worldly manner of

the uncle, than by the incomprehensible allusion to the young noblemen under his tuition.

" Look here, sir," said Ralph ; " I'll put this matter in its true light in two seconds."

" If you'll have the goodness," rejoined Squeers.

" This is a boy, or a youth, or a lad, or a young man, or a hobbledehoy, or whatever you like to call him, of eighteen or nineteen, or thereabouts," said Ralph.

" That I see," observed the schoolmaster.

" So do I," said Mr. Snawley, thinking it as well to back his new friend occasionally.

" His father is dead, he is wholly ignorant of the world, has no resources whatever, and wants something to do," said Ralph. " I recommend him to this splendid establishment of yours as an opening which will lead him to fortune if he turns it to proper account. Do you see that ? "

" Everybody must see that," replied Squeers, half imitating the sneer with which the old gentleman was regarding his unconscious relative.

" I do, of course," said Nicholas, eagerly.

" He does, of course, you observe," said Ralph, in the same dry, hard manner. " If any caprice of temper should induce him to cast aside this golden opportunity before he has brought it to perfection, I consider myself absolved from extending any assistance to his mother and sister. Look at him, and think of the use he may be to you in half a dozen ways ! Now, the question is, whether, for some time to come at all events, he won't serve your purpose better than twenty of the kind of people you would get under ordinary circumstances. Isn't that a question for consideration ? "

" Yes, it is," said Squeers, answering a nod of Ralph's head with a nod of his own.

" Good," rejoined Ralph. " Let me have two words with you."

The two words were had apart ; in a couple of minutes Mr. Wackford Squeers announced that Mr. Nicholas Nickleby was, from that moment, thoroughly nominated to, and installed in, the office of first assistant master at Dotheboys Hall.

" Your uncle's recommendation has done it, Mr. Nickleby," said Wackford Squeers.

Nicholas, overjoyed at his success, shook his uncle's hand warmly, and could almost have worshipped Squeers upon the spot.

" He is an odd-looking man," thought Nicholas. " What of that ?   Porson was an odd-looking man, and so was Doctor Johnson ; all these bookworms are."

" At eight o'clock to-morrow morning, Mr. Nickleby," said Squeers, " the coach starts. You must be here at a quarter before, as we take these boys with us."

" Certainly, sir," said Nicholas.

" And your fare down, I have paid," growled Ralph. " So you'll have nothing to do but keep yourself warm."

Here was another instance of his uncle's generosity ! Nicholas felt his unexpected kindness so much that he could scarcely find words to thank him ; indeed, he had not found half enough, when they took leave of the schoolmaster, and emerged from the Saracen's Head gateway.

Charles Dickens (1812–1870).

From " Nicholas Nickleby."

A Year in the Life of Cromwell

1631

In or soon after 1631, as we laboriously infer from the imbroglio records of poor Noble, Oliver decided on

an enlarged sphere of action as a Farmer ; sold his
properties in Huntingdon, all or some of them ; rented
certain grazing-lands at St. Ives, five miles down the
River, eastward of his native place, and removed thither.
The Deed of Sale is dated 7th May 1631 ; the properties
are specified as in the possession of himself or his Mother ;
the sum they yielded was 1800*l*. With this sum Oliver
stocked his Grazing-Farm at St. Ives. The Mother, we
infer, continued to reside at Huntingdon, but with-
drawn now from active occupation into the retirement
befitting a widow up in years. There is even some
gleam of evidence to that effect : her properties are
sold ; but Oliver's children born to him at St. Ives are
still christened at Huntingdon, in the Church he was
used to ; which may mean also that their good Grand-
mother was still there.

Properly this was no change in Oliver's old activities ;
it was an enlargement of the sphere of them. His
Mother still at Huntingdon, within few miles of him, he
could still superintend and protect her existence there,
while managing his new operations at St. Ives. He
continued here till the summer or spring of 1636. A
studious imagination may sufficiently construct the
figure of his equable life in those years. Diligent grass-
farming, mowing, milking, cattle-marketing : add
" hypochondria," fits of the blackness of darkness,
with glances of the brightness of very Heaven ; prayer,
religious reading and meditation, household epochs, joys
and cares :—we have a solid, substantial, inoffensive
Farmer of St. Ives, hoping to walk with integrity and
humble devout diligence through this world ; and, by
his Maker's infinite mercy, to escape destruction, and
find eternal salvation in wider Divine Worlds. This
latter, this is the grand clause in his Life, which dwarfs
all other clauses. Much wider destinies than he antici-
pated were appointed him on Earth ; but that, in com-

parison to the alternative of Heaven or Hell to all
Eternity, was a mighty small matter.

The lands he rented are still there, recognizable to
the Tourist ; gross boggy lands, fringed with willow-
trees, at the east end of the small Town of St. Ives,
which is still noted as a cattle-market in those parts.
The " Cromwell Barn," the pretended " House of Cromwell," the &c. &c. are, as is usual in these cases, when
you come to try them by the documents, a mere jumble
of incredibilities, and oblivious human platitudes, distressing to the mind.

Thomas Carlyle (1795–1881).

From " The Life of Oliver Cromwell."

Early Times in England

Nothing in the early existence of Britain indicated
the greatness which she was destined to attain. Her
inhabitants, when first they became known to the Tyrian
mariners, were little superior to the natives of the Sand-
wich Islands. She was subjugated by the Roman arms ;
but she received only a faint tincture of Roman arts
and letters. Of the western provinces which obeyed
the Cæsars she was the last that was conquered, and
the first that was flung away. No magnificent remains
of Latian porches and aqueducts are to be found in
Britain. No writer of British birth is reckoned among
the masters of Latian poetry and eloquence. It is not
probable that the islanders were at any time generally
familiar with the tongue of their Italian rulers. From
the Atlantic to the vicinity of the Rhine the Latin has,
during many centuries, been predominant. It drove
out the Celtic ; it was not driven out by the Teutonic ;
and it is at this day the basis of the French, Spanish,

and Portuguese languages. In our island the Latin appears never to have superseded the old Gaelic speech, and could not stand its ground against the German.

The scanty and superficial civilization which the Britons had derived from their southern masters was effaced by the calamities of the fifth century. In the continental kingdoms into which the Roman empire was then dissolved, the conquerors learned much from the conquered race. In Britain the conquered race became as barbarous as the conquerors.

All the chiefs who founded Teutonic dynasties in the continental provinces of the Roman empire, Alaric, Theodoric, Clovis, Alboin, were zealous Christians. The followers of Ida and Cerdic, on the other hand, brought to their settlements in Britain all the superstitions of the Elbe. While the German princes who reigned at Paris, Toledo, Arles, and Ravenna listened with reverence to the instructions of bishops, adored the relics of martyrs, and took part eagerly in disputes touching the Nicene theology, the rulers of Wessex and Mercia were still performing savage rites in the temples of Thor and Woden.

The continental kingdoms which had risen on the ruins of the Western Empire kept up some intercourse with those eastern provinces where the ancient civilization, though slowly fading away under the influence of misgovernment, might still astonish and instruct barbarians, where the court still exhibited the splendour of Diocletian and Constantine, where the public buildings were still adorned with the sculptures of Polycletus and the paintings of Apelles, and where laborious pedants, themselves destitute of taste, sense, and spirit, could still read and interpret the masterpieces of Sophocles, of Demosthenes, and of Plato. From this communion Britain was cut off. Her shores were, to the polished race which dwelt by the Bosporus, objects of a mys-

terious horror, such as that with which the Ionians of
the age of Homer had regarded the Straits of Scylla
and the city of the Læstrygonian cannibals. There was
one province of our island in which, as Procopius had
been told, the ground was covered with serpents, and
the air was such that no man could inhale it and live.
To this desolate region the spirits of the departed were
ferried over from the land of the Franks at midnight.
A strange race of fishermen performed the ghastly office.
The speech of the dead was distinctly heard by the
boatmen : their weight made the keel sink deep in the
water ; but their forms were invisible to mortal eye.
Such were the marvels which an able historian, the
contemporary of Belisarius, of Simplicius, and of Tri-
bonian, gravely related in the rich and polite Constantinople, touching the country in which the founder of
Constantinople had assumed the imperial purple. Con-
cerning all the other provinces of the Western Empire
we have continuous information. It is only in Britain
that an age of fable completely separates two ages of
truth. Odoacer and Totila, Euric and Thrasimund,
Clovis, Fredegunda, and Brunechild, are historical men
and women. But Hengist and Horsa, Vortigern and
Rowena, Arthur and Mordred are mythical persons,
whose very existence may be questioned, and whose
adventures must be classed with those of Hercules and
Romulus.

At length the darkness begins to break ; and the country which had been lost to view as Britain reappears
as England. The conversion of the Saxon colonists to
Christianity was the first of a long series of salutary
revolutions. It is true that the Church had been deeply
corrupted both by that superstition and by that philosophy against which she had long contended, and over
which she had at last triumphed. She had given a too
easy admission to doctrines borrowed from the ancient

schools, and to rites borrowed from the ancient temples.
Roman policy and Gothic ignorance, Grecian ingenuity
and Syrian asceticism, had contributed to deprave her.
Yet she retained enough of the sublime theology and
benevolent morality of her earlier days to elevate many
intellects, and to purify many hearts. Some things
also which at a later period were justly regarded as
among her chief blemishes were, in the seventh century,
and long afterwards, among her chief merits. That
the sacerdotal order should encroach on the functions
of the civil magistrate would, in our time, be a great
evil. But that which in an age of good government
is an evil may, in an age of grossly bad government,
be a blessing. It is better that mankind should be
governed by wise laws well administered, and by an
enlightened public opinion, than by priestcraft : but it
is better that men should be governed by priestcraft
than by brute violence, by such a prelate as Dunstan
than by such a warrior as Penda. A society sunk in
ignorance, and ruled by mere physical force, has great
reason to rejoice when a class, of which the influence
is intellectual and moral, rises to ascendency. Such a
class will doubtless abuse its power : but mental power,
even when abused, is still a nobler and better power
than that which consists merely in corporeal strength.
We read in our Saxon chronicles of tyrants, who, when
at the height of greatness, were smitten with remorse,
who abhorred the pleasure and dignities which they
had purchased by guilt, who abdicated their crowns,
and who sought to atone for their offences by cruel
penances and incessant prayers. These stories have
drawn forth bitter expressions of contempt from some
writers who, while they boasted of liberality, were in
truth as narrow-minded as any monk of the dark ages,
and whose habit was to apply to all events in the history of the world the standard received in the Parisian

society of the eighteenth century. Yet surely a system which, however deformed by superstition, introduced strong moral restraints into communities previously governed only by vigour of muscle and by audacity of spirit, a system which taught the fiercest and mightiest ruler that he was, like his meanest bondman, a responsible being, might have seemed to deserve a more respectful mention from philosophers and philanthropists.

The same observations will apply to the contempt with which, in the last century, it was fashionable to speak of the pilgrimages, the sanctuaries, the crusades, and the monastic institutions of the middle ages. In times when men were scarcely ever induced to travel by liberal curiosity, or by the pursuit of gain, it was better that the rude inhabitant of the North should visit Italy and the East as a pilgrim, than that he should never see anything but those squalid cabins and uncleared woods amidst which he was born. In times when life and when female honour were exposed to daily risk from tyrants and marauders, it was better that the precinct of a shrine should be regarded with an irrational awe, than that there should be no refuge inaccessible to cruelty and licentiousness. In times when statesmen were incapable of forming extensive political combinations, it was better that the Christian nations should be roused and united for the recovery of the Holy Sepulchre, than that they should, one by one, be overwhelmed by the Mahometan power. Whatever reproach may, at a later period, have been justly thrown on the indolence and luxury of religious orders, it was surely good that, in an age of ignorance and violence, there should be quiet cloisters and gardens, in which the arts of peace could be safely cultivated, in which gentle and contemplative natures could find an asylum, in which one brother could employ himself in transcribing the Æneid of Virgil, and another in meditating the Analytics of Aristotle, in which he who had a genius for art might illuminate a martyrology or carve a crucifix, and in which he who had a turn for natural philosophy might make experiments on the properties of plants and minerals. Had not such retreats been scattered here and there, among the huts of a miserable peasantry, and the castles of a ferocious aristocracy, European society would have consisted merely of beasts of burden and beasts of prey. The Church has many times been compared by divines to the ark of which we read in the Book of Genesis : but never was the resemblance more perfect than during that evil time when she alone rode, amidst darkness and tempest, on the deluge beneath which all the great works of ancient power and wisdom lay entombed, bearing within her that feeble germ from which a second and more glorious civilization was to spring.

Even the spiritual supremacy arrogated by the Pope was, in the dark ages, productive of far more good than evil. Its effect was to unite the nations of Western Europe in one great commonwealth. What the Olympian chariot course and the Pythian oracle were to all the Greek cities, from Trebizond to Marseilles, Rome and her Bishop were to all Christians of the Latin communion, from Calabria to the Hebrides. Thus grew up sentiments of enlarged benevolence. Races separated from each other by seas and mountains acknowledged a fraternal tie and a common code of public law. Even in war, the cruelty of the conqueror was not seldom mitigated by the recollection that he and his vanquished enemies were all members of one great federation.

Into this federation our Saxon ancestors were now admitted. A regular communication was opened between our shores and that part of Europe in which the traces of ancient power and policy were yet discernible. Many noble monuments which have since been destroyed or defaced still retained their pristine magnificence; and travellers, to whom Livy and Sallust were unintelligible, might gain from the Roman aqueducts and temples some faint notion of Roman history. The dome of Agrippa, still glittering with bronze, the mausoleum of Adrian, not yet deprived of its columns and statues, the Flavian amphitheatre, not yet degraded into a quarry, told to the rude English pilgrims some part of the story of that great civilized world which had passed away. The islanders returned, with awe deeply impressed on their half opened minds, and told the wondering inhabitants of the hovels of London and York that, near the grave of St. Peter, a mighty race, now extinct, had piled up buildings which would never be dissolved till the judgment day. Learning followed in the train of Christianity. The poetry and eloquence of the Augustan age was assiduously studied in Mercian and Northumbrian monasteries. The names of Bede, of Alcuin, and of John, surnamed Erigena, were justly celebrated throughout Europe. Such was the state of our country when, in the ninth century, began the last great descent of the northern barbarians.

During several generations Denmark and Scandinavia continued to pour forth innumerable pirates, distinguished by strength, by valour, by merciless ferocity, and by hatred of the Christian name. No country suffered so much from these invaders as England. Her coast lay near to the ports whence they sailed; nor was any part of our island so far distant from the sea as to be secure from attack. The same atrocities which had attended the victory of the Saxon over the Celt were now, after the lapse of ages, suffered by the Saxon at the hand of the Dane. Civilization, just as it began to rise, was met by this blow, and sank down once more. Large colonies of adventurers from the Baltic established themselves on the eastern shores, spread gradually

K

westward, and, supported by constant reinforcements from beyond the sea, aspired to the dominion of the whole realm. The struggle between the two fierce Teutonic breeds lasted during six generations. Each was alternately paramount. Cruel massacres followed by cruel retribution, provinces wasted, convents plundered, and cities rased to the ground, make up the greater part of the history of those evil days. At length the North ceased to send forth a constant stream of fresh depredators, and from that time the mutual aversion of the races began to subside. Intermarriage became frequent. The Danes learned the religion of the Saxons; and thus one cause of deadly animosity was removed. The Danish and Saxon tongues, both dialects of one widespread language, were blended together. But the distinction between the two nations was by no means effaced, when an event took place which prostrated both, in common slavery and degradation, at the feet of a third people.

The Normans were then the foremost race of Christendom. Their valour and ferocity had made them conspicuous among the rovers whom Scandinavia had sent forth to ravage Western Europe. Their sails were long the terror of both coasts of the channel. Their arms were repeatedly carried far into the heart of the Carlovingian empire, and were victorious under the walls of Maestricht and Paris. At length one of the feeble heirs of Charlemagne ceded to the strangers a fertile province, watered by a noble river, and contiguous to the sea which was their favourite element. In that province they founded a mighty state, which gradually extended its influence over the neighbouring principalities of Brittany and Maine. Without laying aside that dauntless valour which had been the terror of every land from the Elbe to the Pyrenees, the Normans rapidly acquired all, and more than all, the knowledge and refinement

which they found in the country where they settled.
Their courage secured their territory against foreign
invasion. They established internal order, such as had
long been unknown in the Frank empire. They em-
braced Christianity, and with Christianity they learned
a great part of what the clergy had to teach. They
abandoned their native speech, and adopted the French
tongue, in which the Latin was the predominant element.
They speedily raised their new language to a dignity
and importance which it had never before possessed.
They found it a barbarous jargon; they fixed it in
writing; and they employed it in legislation, in poetry,
and in romance. They renounced that brutal intemper-
ance to which all the other branches of the great German family were too much inclined. The polite luxury
of the Norman presented a striking contrast to the
coarse voracity and drunkenness of his Saxon and Danish
neighbours. He loved to display his magnificence, not
in huge piles of food and hogsheads of strong drink,
but in large and stately edifices, rich armour, gallant
horses, choice falcons, well ordered tournaments, ban-
quets delicate rather than abundant, and wines remarkable rather for their exquisite flavour than for their
intoxicating power. That chivalrous spirit, which has
exercised so powerful an influence on the politics, morals,
and manners of all the European nations, was found
in the highest exaltation among the Norman nobles.
Those nobles were distinguished by their graceful bearing and insinuating address. They were distinguished
also by their skill in negotiation, and by a natural
eloquence which they assiduously cultivated. It was
the boast of one of their historians that the Norman
gentlemen were orators from the cradle. But their
chief fame was derived from their military exploits.
Every country, from the Atlantic Ocean to the Dead
Sea, witnessed the prodigies of their discipline and

valour. One Norman knight, at the head of a handful of warriors, scattered the Celts of Connaught. Another founded the monarchy of the Two Sicilies, and saw the emperors both of the East and of the West fly before his arms. A third, the Ulysses of the first crusade, was invested by his fellow soldiers with the sovereignty of Antioch ; and a fourth, the Tancred whose name lives in the great poem of Tasso, was celebrated through Christendom as the bravest and most generous of the champions of the Holy Sepulchre.

The vicinity of so remarkable a people early began to produce an effect on the public mind of England. Before the Conquest, English princes received their education in Normandy. English sees and English estates were bestowed on Normans. The French of Normandy was familiarly spoken in the palace of Westminster. The court of Rouen seems to have been to the court of Edward the Confessor what the court of Versailles long afterwards was to the court of Charles the Second.

Thomas Babington, Lord Macaulay (1800–1859).

From " The History of England," Chapter I.

A Boy's Adventure

The cave proved a mine of wonders. We found it of great depth, and when at its farthest extremity, the sea and opposite land appeared to us as they would if viewed through the tube of a telescope. We discovered that its sides and roof were crusted over with a white stone resembling marble, and that it contained a petrifying spring. The pigeons which we disturbed were whizzing by us through the gloom, reminding us of the hags of our story books, when on their night voyage

through the air. A shoal of porpoises were tempesting
the water in their unwieldy gambols, scarcely an hundred yards from the cavern's mouth, and a flock of sea-
gulls were screaming around them, like harpies round
the viands of the Trojan. To add to the interest of
the place, we had learned from tradition that, *in the
lang syne*, this cave had furnished Wallace with a hiding-
place, and that more recently it had been haunted by
smugglers. In the midst of our engagements, however,
the evening began to darken; and we discovered that
our very fine cave was neither more nor less than a
prison. We attempted climbing round, but in vain;
for the shelf from whence we had leaped was unattain-
able, and there was no other path. "What will my
mother think?" said the poor little fellow whom I had
brought into this predicament, as he burst into tears.
"I would care nothing for myself—but my mother."
The appeal was powerful, and, had he not cried, I probably would; but the sight of his tears roused my pride,
and, with a feeling which Rochefoucault would have at
once recognized as springing from the master principle,
I attempted to comfort him; and for the time completely
forgot my own sorrow in exulting, with all due sympathy, over his. Night came on both dark and rainy,
and we lay down together in a corner of the cave. A
few weeks prior, the corpse of a fisherman, who had
been drowned early in the preceding winter, had been
found on the beach below. It was much gashed by
the sharp rocks, and the head was beaten to pieces. I
had seen it at the time it was carried through the streets
of Cromarty to the church, where in this part of the
country the bodies of drowned persons are commonly
put until the coffin and grave be prepared; and all this
night long, sleeping or waking, the image of this corpse
was continually before me. As often as I slumbered, a
mangled headless thing would come stalking into the

cave and attempt striking me, when I would awaken
with a start, cling to my companion, and hide my face
in his breast. About one o'clock in the morning we
were relieved by two boats, which our friends, who had
spent the early part of the night in searching for us in
the woods above, had fitted out to try along the shore
for our bodies; they having at length concluded that
we had fallen over the cliffs, and were killed.

[*When much older, Hugh Miller " put in the sky " of
the picture in the following manner :*] The sun had sunk
behind the precipices, and all was gloom along their
bases, and double gloom in their caves; but their rugged
brows still caught the red glare of evening. The flush
rose higher and higher, chased by the shadows; and
then, after lingering for a moment on their crests of
honeysuckle and juniper, passed away, and the whole
became sombre and grey. The sea-gull sprang upward
from where he had floated on the ripple, and hied him
slowly away to his lodge in his deep-sea stack; the
dusky cormorant flitted past, with heavier and more
frequent stroke, to his whitened shelf high on the precipice; the pigeons came whizzing downwards from the
uplands and the opposite land, and disappeared amid
the gloom of their caves; every creature that had wings
made use of them in speeding homewards; but neither
my companion nor myself had any; and there was no
possibility of getting home without them. . . . For
the last few hours mountainous piles of clouds had been
rising dark and stormy in the sea-mouth : they had
flared portentously in the setting sun, and had worn,
with the decline of evening, almost every meteoric tint
of anger, from fiery red to a sombre thundrous brown,
and from sombre brown to doleful black.

Hugh Miller (1802–1856).

From Bayne's " Life and Letters of Hugh Miller."

Troublous Times

Not having been able to sleep, for thinking of some lines for eels which he had placed the night before, the lad was lying in his little bed, waiting for the hour when the gate would be open, and he and his comrade, John Lockwood, the porter's son, might go to the pond and see what fortune had brought them. At daybreak, John was to awaken him, but his own eagerness for the sport had served as a *réveillez* long since—so long, that it seemed to him as if the day never would come.

It might have been four o'clock when he heard the door of the opposite chamber, the Chaplain's room, open, and the voice of a man coughing in the passage. Harry jumped up, thinking for certain it was a robber, or hoping perhaps for a ghost, and, flinging open his own door, saw before him the Chaplain's door open, and a light inside, and a figure standing in the doorway, in the midst of a great smoke which issued from the room.

" Who's there ? " cried out the boy, who was of a good spirit.

" *Silentium !* " whispered the other ; " 'tis I, my boy ! " and, holding his hand out, Harry had no difficulty in recognizing his master and friend, Father Holt. A curtain was over the window of the Chaplain's room that looked to the court, and Harry saw that the smoke came from a great flame of papers which were burning in a brazier when he entered the Chaplain's room. After giving a hasty greeting and blessing to the lad, who was charmed to see his tutor, the Father continued the burning of his papers, drawing them from a cupboard over the mantelpiece wall, which Harry had never seen before.

Father Holt laughed, seeing the lad's attention fixed at once on this hole. " That is right, Harry," he said ;

" faithful little famuli see all and say nothing. You
are faithful, I know."

" I know I would go to the stake for you," said Harry.

" I don't want your head," said the Father, patting
it kindly ; " all you have to do is to hold your tongue.
Let us burn these papers, and say nothing to anybody.
Should you like to read them ? "

Harry Esmond blushed, and held down his head ;
he *had* looked as the fact was, and without thinking,
at the paper before him; and though he had seen it,
could not understand a word of it, the letters being
quite clear enough, but quite without meaning. They
burned the papers, beating down the ashes in a brazier,
so that scarce any traces of them remained.

Harry had been accustomed to see Father Holt in
more dresses than one ; it not being safe, or worth the
danger, for Popish ecclesiastics to wear their proper
dress ; and he was, in consequence, in no wise astonished
that the priest should now appear before him in a riding
dress, with large buff leather boots, and a feather to
his hat, plain, but such as gentlemen wore.

" You know the secret of the cupboard," said he,
laughing, " and must be prepared for other mysteries ; "
and he opened—but not a secret cupboard this time—
only a wardrobe, which he usually kept locked, and
from which he now took out two or three dresses and
perruques of different colours, and a couple of swords
of a pretty make (Father Holt was an expert practitioner
with the small-sword, and every day, whilst he was at
home, he and his pupil practised this exercise, in which
the lad became a very great proficient), a military coat
and cloak, and a farmer's smock, and placed them in
the large hole over the mantelpiece from which the
papers had been taken.

" If they miss the cupboard," he said, " they will not
find these ; if they find them, they'll tell no tales, except

that Father Holt wore more suits of clothes than one.
All Jesuits do. You know what deceivers we are,
Harry."

Harry was alarmed at the notion that his friend was
about to leave him; but "No," the priest said, "I
may very likely come back with my Lord in a few days.
We are to be tolerated; we are not to be persecuted.
But they may take a fancy to pay a visit at Castlewood
ere our return; and, as gentlemen of my cloth are sus-
pected, they might choose to examine my papers, which
concern nobody—at least not them." And to this day,
whether the papers in cipher related to politics, or to
the affairs of that mysterious society whereof Father
Holt was a member, his pupil, Harry Esmond, remains
in entire ignorance.

The rest of his goods, his small wardrobe, &c., Holt
left untouched on his shelves and in his cupboard, taking down—with a laugh, however—and flinging into
the brazier, where he only half burned them, some
theological treatises which he had been writing against
the English divines. "And now," said he, "Henry,
my son, you may testify, with a safe conscience, that
you saw me burning Latin sermons the last time I was
here before I went away to London; and it will be daybreak directly, and I must be away before Lockwood
is stirring."

"Will not Lockwood let you out, sir?" Esmond
asked. Holt laughed; he was never more gay or good-
humoured than when in the midst of action or danger.

"Lockwood knows nothing of my being here, mind
you," he said; "nor would you, you little wretch!
had you slept better. You must forget that I have
been here; and now farewell. Close the door, and go
to your own room, and don't come out till—stay, why
should you not know one secret more? I know you
will never betray me."

In the Chaplain's room were two windows : the one looking into the court facing westwards to the fountain ; the other, a small casement strongly barred, and looking on to the green in front of the Hall. This window was too high to reach from the ground : but, mounting on a buffet which stood beneath it, Father Holt showed me how, by pressing on the base of the window, the whole framework of lead, glass, and iron stanchions descended into a cavity worked below, from which it could be drawn and restored to its usual place from without ; a broken pane being purposely open to admit the hand which was to work upon the spring of the machine.

"When I am gone," Father Holt said, "you may push away the buffet, so that no one may fancy that an exit has been made that way ; lock the door ; place the key—where shall we put the key ?—under ' Chrysostom ' on the bookshelf ; and if any ask for it, say I keep it there, and told you where to find it, if you had need to go to my room. The descent is easy down the wall into the ditch ; and so once more farewell, until I see thee again, my dear son." And with this the intrepid Father mounted the buffet with great agility and briskness, stepped across the window, lifting up the bars and framework again from the other side, and only leaving room for Harry Esmond to stand on tiptoe and kiss his hand before the casement closed, the bars fixing as firm as ever, seemingly, in the stone arch overhead. When Father Holt next arrived at Castlewood, it was by the public gate on horseback ; and he never so much as alluded to the existence of the private issue to Harry, except when he had need of a private messenger from within, for which end, no doubt, he had instructed his young pupil in the means of quitting the Hall.

Esmond, young as he was, would have died sooner

than betray his friend and master, as Mr. Holt well
knew ; for he had tried the boy more than once, putting temptations in his way, to see whether he would
yield to them and confess afterwards, or whether he
would resist them, as he did sometimes, or whether he
would lie, which he never did. Holt instructing the
boy on this point, however, that if to keep silence is
not to lie, as it certainly is not, yet silence is, after all,
equivalent to a negation—and therefore a downright
No, in the interest of justice or your friend, and in reply
to a question that may be prejudicial to either, is not
criminal, but, on the contrary, praiseworthy ; and as
lawful a way as the other of eluding a wrongful demand.
For instance (says he), suppose a good citizen, who had
seen His Majesty take refuge there, had been asked,
" Is King Charles up that oak-tree ? " his duty would
have been not to say, Yes—so that the Cromwellians
should seize the King and murder him like his father—
but No ; His Majesty being private in the tree, and
therefore not to be seen there by loyal eyes : all which
instruction, in religion and morals, as well as in the
rudiments of the tongues and sciences, the boy took
eagerly and with gratitude from his tutor. When, then,
Holt was gone, and told Harry not to see him, it was
as if he had never been. And he had this answer pat
when he came to be questioned a few days after.

The Prince of Orange was then at Salisbury, as young
Esmond learned from seeing Doctor Tusher in his best
cassock (though the roads were muddy, and he never
was known to wear his silk, only his stuff one, a-horse-
back), with a great orange cockade in his broad-leafed
hat, and Nahum, his clerk, ornamented with a like
decoration. The Doctor was walking up and down in
front of his parsonage, when little Esmond saw him,
and heard him say he was going to pay his duty to his
Highness the Prince, as he mounted his pad and rode

away with Nahum behind. The village people had
orange cockades too, and his friend the blacksmith's
laughing daughter pinned one into Harry's old hat,
which he tore out indignantly when they bade him to
cry " God save the Prince of Orange and the Protestant
religion ! " but the people only laughed, for they liked
the boy in the village, where his solitary condition moved
the general pity, and where he found friendly welcomes
and faces in many houses. Father Holt had many
friends there too, for he not only would fight the blacksmith at theology, never losing his temper, but laughing
the whole time in his pleasant way ; but he cured him
of an ague with quinquina, and was always ready with
a kind word for any man that asked it, so that they
said in the village 'twas a pity the two were Papists.

The Director and the Vicar of Castlewood agreed
very well ; indeed, the former was a perfectly-bred
gentleman, and it was the latter's business to agree
with everybody. Doctor Tusher and the lady's-maid,
his spouse, had a boy who was about the age of little
Esmond ; and there was such a friendship between the
lads, as propinquity and tolerable kindness and good-
humour on either side would be pretty sure to occasion.
Tom Tusher was sent off early, however, to a school in
London, whither his father took him and a volume of
sermons, in the first year of the reign of King James ;
and Tom returned but once a year afterwards to Castlewood for many years of his scholastic and collegiate
life. Thus there was less danger to Tom of a perversion
of his faith by the Director, who scarce ever saw him,
than there was to Harry, who constantly was in the
Vicar's company ; but as long as Harry's religion was
His Majesty's, and my Lord's, and my Lady's, the
Doctor said gravely, it should not be for him to disturb
or disquiet him : it was far from him to say that His
Majesty's Church was not a branch of the Catholic

Church; upon which Father Holt used, according to his custom, to laugh, and say that the Holy Church throughout all the world, and the noble Army of Martyrs, were very much obliged to the Doctor.

It was while Doctor Tusher was away at Salisbury that there came a troop of dragoons with orange scarfs, and quartered in Castlewood, and some of them came up to the Hall, where they took possession, robbing nothing however beyond the hen-house and the beer-cellar; and only insisting upon going through the house and looking for papers. The first room they asked to look at was Father Holt's room, of which Harry Esmond brought the key, and they opened the drawers and the cupboards, and tossed over the papers and clothes— but found nothing except his books and clothes, and the vestments in a box by themselves, with which the dragoons made merry, to Harry Esmond's horror. And to the questions which the gentleman put to Harry, he replied that Father Holt was a very kind man to him, and a very learned man, and Harry supposed would tell him none of his secrets, if he had any. He was about eleven years old at this time, and looked as innocent as boys of his age.

The family were away more than six months, and when they returned they were in the deepest state of dejection, for King James had been banished, the Prince of Orange was on the throne, and the direst persecutions of those of the Catholic faith were apprehended by my Lady, who said she did not believe that there was a word of truth in the promises of toleration that Dutch monster made, or in a single word the perjured wretch said. My Lord and Lady were in a manner prisoners in their own house; so her Ladyship gave the little page to know, who was by this time growing of an age to understand what was passing about him, and something of the characters of the people he lived with.

" We are prisoners," says she ; " in everything but chains we are prisoners. Let them come, let them consign me to dungeons, or strike off my head from this poor little throat " (and she clasped it in her long fingers). " The blood of the Esmonds will always flow freely for their kings. We are not like the Churchills—the Judases, who kiss their master and betray him. We know how to suffer, how even to forgive in the royal cause " (no doubt it was that fatal business of losing the place of Groom of the Posset to which her Ladyship alluded, as she did half a dozen times in the day). " Let the tyrant of Orange bring his rack and his odious Dutch tortures —the beast ! the wretch ! I spit upon him and defy him. Cheerfully will I lay this head upon the block ; cheerfully will I accompany my Lord to the scaffold : we will cry ' God save King James ! ' with our dying breath, and smile in the face of the executioner." And she told her page, a hundred times at least, of the particulars of the last interview which she had with His Majesty.

" I flung myself before my liege's feet," she said, " at Salisbury. I devoted myself—my husband—my house, to his cause. Perhaps he remembered old times, when Isabella Esmond was young and fair ; perhaps he recalled the day when 'twas not *I* that knelt—at least he spoke to me with a voice that reminded *me* of days gone by. ' Egad ! ' said His Majesty, ' you should go to the Prince of Orange, if you want anything.' ' No, sire,' I replied, ' I would not kneel to a Usurper ; the Esmond that would have served your Majesty will never be groom to a traitor's posset.' The royal exile smiled, even in the midst of his misfortune ; he deigned to raise me with words of consolation. The Viscount, my husband, himself, could not be angry at the august salute with which he honoured me ! ' "

The public misfortune had the effect of making my

Lord and his Lady better friends than they ever had been since their courtship. My Lord Viscount had shown both loyalty and spirit, when these were rare qualities in the dispirited party about the King; and the praise he got elevated him not a little in his wife's good opinion, and perhaps in his own. He wakened up from the listless and supine life which he had been leading; was always riding to and fro in consultation with this friend or that of the King's; the page of course knowing little of his doings, but remarking only his greater cheerfulness and altered demeanour.

Father Holt came to the Hall constantly, but officiated no longer openly as Chaplain; he was always fetching and carrying: strangers, military and ecclesiastic (Harry knew the latter, though they came in all sorts of disguises), were continually arriving and departing. My Lord made long absences and sudden reappearances, using sometimes the means of exit which Father Holt had employed, though how often the little window in the Chaplain's room let in or let out my Lord and his friends, Harry could not tell. He stoutly kept his promise to the Father of not prying, and if at midnight from his little room he heard noises of persons stirring in the next chamber, he turned round to the wall, and hid his curiosity under his pillow until it fell asleep. Of course he could not help remarking that the priest's journeys were constant, and understanding by a hundred signs that some active though secret business employed him : what this was may pretty well be guessed by what soon happened to my Lord.

No garrison or watch was put into Castlewood when my Lord came back, but a guard was in the village; and one or other of them was always on the Green keeping a look-out on our great gate, and those who went out and in. Lockwood said that at night especially every person who came in or went out was watched by

the outlying sentries. 'Twas lucky that we had a gate
which their Worships knew nothing about. My Lord
and Father Holt must have made constant journeys at
night : once or twice little Harry acted as their messenger and discreet aide-de-camp. He remembers he was
bidden to go into the village with his fishing-rod, enter
certain houses, ask for a drink of water, and tell the
good man, " There would be a horse-market at Newbury
next Thursday," and so carry the same message on to
the next house on his list.

He did not know what the message meant at the
time, nor what was happening : which may as well,
however, for clearness' sake, be explained here. The
Prince of Orange being gone to Ireland, where the King
was ready to meet him with a great army, it was determined that a great rising of His Majesty's party should
take place in this country ; and my Lord was to head
the force in our county. Of late he had taken a greater
lead in affairs than before, having the indefatigable
Mr. Holt at his elbow, and my Lady Viscountess strongly
urging him on ; and my Lord Sark being in the Tower a
prisoner, and Sir Wilmot Crawley, of Queen's Crawley,
having gone over to the Prince of Orange's side—my
Lord became the most considerable person in our part
of the county for the affairs of the King.

It was arranged that the regiment of Scots Greys and
Dragoons, then quartered at Newbury, should declare
for the King on a certain day, when likewise the gentry
affected to His Majesty's cause were to come in with
their tenants and adherents to Newbury, march upon
the Dutch troops at Reading under Ginckel ; and, these
overthrown, and their indomitable little master away
in Ireland, 'twas thought that our side might move on
London itself, and a confident victory was predicted for
the King.

As these great matters were in agitation, my Lord

lost his listless manner and seemed to gain health ; my Lady did not scold him, Mr. Holt came to and fro, busy always ; and little Harry longed to have been a few inches taller, that he might draw a sword in this good cause.

One day, it must have been about the month of June, 1690, my Lord, in a great horseman's coat, under which Harry could see the shining of a steel breastplate he had on, called little Harry to him, put the hair off the child's forehead, and kissed him, and bade God bless him in such an affectionate way as he never had used before. Father Holt blessed him too, and then they took leave of my Lady Viscountess, who came from her apartment with a pocket-handkerchief to her eyes, and her gentlewoman and Mrs. Tusher supporting her. " You are going to—to ride," says she. " Oh, that I might come too !—but in my situation I am forbidden horse exercise."

" We kiss my Lady Marchioness's hand," says Mr. Holt.

" My Lord, God speed you ! " she said, stepping up and embracing my Lord in a grand manner. " Mr. Holt, I ask your blessing ; " and she knelt down for that, whilst Mrs. Tusher tossed her head up.

Mr. Holt gave the same benediction to the little page, who went down and held my Lord's stirrups for him to mount ; there were two servants waiting there too— and they rode out of Castlewood gate.

As they crossed the bridge, Harry could see an officer in scarlet ride up touching his hat, and address my Lord.

The party stopped, and came to some parley or discussion, which presently ended, my Lord putting his horse into a canter after taking off his hat and making a bow to the officer, who rode alongside him step for step : the trooper accompanying him falling back, and

L

riding with my Lord's two men. They cantered over the Green, and behind the elms (my Lord waving his hand, Harry thought), and so they disappeared. That evening we had a great panic, the cow-boy coming at milking-time riding one of our horses, which he had found grazing at the outer park-wall.

All night my Lady Viscountess was in a very quiet and subdued mood. She scarce found fault with anybody; she played at cards for six hours; little page Esmond went to sleep. He prayed for my Lord and the good cause before closing his eyes.

It was quite in the grey of the morning when the porter's bell rang, and old Lockwood, waking up, let in one of my Lord's servants, who had gone with him in the morning, and who returned with a melancholy story. The officer who rode up to my Lord had, it appeared, said to him, that it was his duty to inform his Lordship that he was not under arrest, but under surveillance, and to request him not to ride abroad that day.

My Lord replied that riding was good for his health, that if the Captain chose to accompany him he was welcome; and it was then that he made a bow, and they cantered away together.

When he came on to Wansey Down, my Lord all of a sudden pulled up, and the party came to a halt at the cross-way.

"Sir," says he to the officer, "we are four to two: will you be so kind as to take that road, and leave me to go mine ? "

"Your road is mine, my Lord," says the officer.

"Then "——says my Lord; but he had no time to say more, for the officer, drawing a pistol, snapped it at his Lordship; as at the same moment, Father Holt, drawing a pistol, shot the officer through the head. It was done, and the man dead in an instant of time. The orderly, gazing at the officer, looked scared for a moment, and galloped away for his life.

" Fire ! fire ! " cries out Father Holt, sending another shot after the trooper, but the two servants were too much surprised to use their pieces, and my Lord calling to them to hold their hands, the fellow got away.

" Mr. Holt, *qui pensait à tout*," says Blaise, " gets off his horse, examines the pockets of the dead officer for papers, gives his money to us two, and says, ' The wine is drawn, M. le Marquis '—why did he say Marquis to M. le Vicomte ?—' we must drink it.' "

" The poor gentleman's horse was a better one than that I rode," Blaise continues : " Mr. Holt bids me get on him, and so I gave a cut to Whitefoot, and she trotted home. We rode on towards Newbury ; we heard firing towards midday : at two o'clock a horseman comes up to us as we were giving our cattle water at an inn—and says, ' All is done ! The Ecossais declared an hour too soon—General Ginckel was down upon them.' The whole thing was at an end."

" ' And we've shot an officer on duty, and let his orderly escape,' says my Lord."

" ' Blaise,' says Mr. Holt, writing two lines on his table-book, one for my Lady, and one for you, Master Harry ; ' you must go back to Castlewood, and deliver these,' and behold me."

And he gave Harry the two papers. He read that to himself, which only said, " Burn the papers in the cupboard, burn this. You know nothing about anything." Harry read this, ran upstairs to his mistress's apartment, where her gentlewoman slept near to the door, made her bring a light and wake my Lady, into whose hands he gave the paper. She was a wonderful object to look at in her night attire, nor had Harry ever seen the like.

As soon as she had the paper in her hand, Harry

stepped back to the Chaplain's room, opened the secret cupboard over the fireplace, burned all the papers in it, and, as he had seen the priest do before, took down one of his reverence's manuscript sermons, and half-burnt that in the brazier. By the time the papers were quite destroyed it was daylight. Harry ran back to his mistress again. Her gentlewoman ushered him again into her Ladyship's chamber ; she told him (from behind her nuptial curtains) to bid the coach be got ready, and that she would ride away anon.

But the mysteries of her Ladyship's toilet were as awfully long on this day as on any other, and, long after the coach was ready, my Lady was still attiring herself. And just as the Viscountess stepped forth from her room, ready for departure, young John Lockwood comes running up from the village with news that a lawyer, three officers, and twenty or four-and-twenty soldiers, were marching thence upon the house. John had but two minutes the start of them, and, ere he had well told his story, the troop rode into our courtyard.

William Makepeace Thackeray (1811–1863.)

From " The History of Henry Esmond," Chapter V.

Boys Together

A playfellow of Richard's occasionally, and the only comrade of his age that he ever saw, was Master Ripton Thompson, the son of Sir Austin's solicitor, a boy without a character.

A comrade of some description was necessary, for Richard was neither to go to school nor to college.

* * * * *

October shone royally on Richard's fourteenth birth-

day. The brown beechwoods and golden birches glowed
to a brilliant sun. Banks of moveless cloud hung about
the horizon, mounded to the west, where slept the wind.
Promise of a great day for Raynham, as it proved to
be, though not in the manner marked out.

Already archery-booths and cricketing-tents were
rising on the lower grounds towards the river, whither
the lads of Bursley and Lobourne, in boats and in carts,
shouting for a day of ale and honour, jogged merrily
to match themselves anew, and pluck at the living laurel
from each other's brows, like manly Britons. The whole
park was beginning to be astir and resound with holi-
day cries. Sir Austin Feverel, a thorough good Tory,
was no game-preserver, and could be popular whenever
he chose, which Sir Miles Papworth, on the other side
of the river, a fast-handed Whig and terror to poachers,
never could be. Half the village of Lobourne was seen
trooping through the avenues of the park. Fiddlers
and gipsies clamoured at the gates for admission : white
smocks, and slate, surmounted by hats of serious brim,
and now and then a scarlet cloak, smacking of the old
country, dotted the grassy sweeps to the levels.

And all the time the star of these festivities was
receding further and further, and eclipsing himself with
his reluctant serf Ripton, who kept asking what they
were to do and where they were going, and how late it
was in the day, and suggesting that the lads of Lobourne
would be calling out for them, and Sir Austin requiring
their presence, without getting any attention paid to
his misery or remonstrances. For Richard had been
requested by his father to submit to medical examina-
tion like a boor enlisting for a soldier, and he was in
great wrath.

He was flying as though he would have flown from
the shameful thought of what had been asked of him.
By and by he communicated his sentiments to Ripton,

who said they were those of a girl : an offensive remark, remembering which, Richard, after they had borrowed a couple of guns at the bailiff's farm, and Ripton had fired badly, called his friend a fool.

Feeling that circumstances were making him look wonderfully like one, Ripton lifted his head and retorted defiantly, " I'm not ! "

This angry contradiction, so very uncalled for, annoyed Richard, who was still smarting at the loss of the birds, owing to Ripton's bad shot, and was really the injured party. He therefore bestowed the abusive epithet on Ripton anew, and with increase of emphasis.

" You shan't call me so, then, whether I am or not," says Ripton, and sucks his lips.

This was becoming personal. Richard sent up his brows, and stared at his defier an instant. He then informed him that he certainly should call him so, and would not object to call him so twenty times.

" Do it, and see ! " returns Ripton, rocking on his feet, and breathing quick.

With a gravity of which only boys and other barbarians are capable, Richard went through the entire number, stressing the epithet to increase the defiance and avoid monotony, as he progressed, while Ripton bobbed his head every time in assent, as it were, to his comrade's accuracy, and as a record for his profound humiliation. The dog they had with them gazed at the extraordinary performance with interrogating wags of the tail.

Twenty times, duly and deliberately, Richard repeated the obnoxious word.

At the twentieth solemn iteration of Ripton's capital shortcoming, Ripton delivered a smart back-hander on Richard's mouth, and squared precipitately ; perhaps sorry when the deed was done, for he was a kind-hearted lad, and as Richard simply bowed in acknowledgment of the blow he thought he had gone too far. He did not know the young gentleman he was dealing with. Richard was extremely cool.

" Shall we fight here ? " he said.

" Anywhere you like," replied Ripton.

" A little more into the wood, I think. We may be interrupted." And Richard led the way with a courteous reserve that somewhat chilled Ripton's ardour for the contest. On the skirts of the wood, Richard threw off his jacket and waistcoat, and, quite collected, waited for Ripton to do the same. The latter boy was flushed and restless ; older and broader, but not so tight-limbed and well-set. The Gods, sole witnesses of their battle, betted dead against him. Richard had mounted the white cockade of the Feverels, and there was a look in him that asked for tough work to extinguish. His brows, slightly lined upward at the temples, converging to a knot about the well-set straight nose ; his full grey eyes, open nostrils, and planted feet, and a gentlemanly air of calm and alertness, formed a spirited picture of a young combatant. As for Ripton, he was all abroad, and fought in school-boy style—that is, he rushed at the foe head foremost, and struck like a windmill. He was a lumpy boy. When he did hit, he made himself felt ; but he was at the mercy of science. To see him come dashing in, blinking and puffing and whirling his arms abroad while the felling blow went straight between them, you perceived that he was fighting a fight of desperation, and knew it. For the dreaded alternative glared him in the face that, if he yielded, he must look like what he had been twenty times calumniously called ; and he would die rather than yield, and swing his windmill till he dropped. Poor boy ! he dropped frequently. The gallant fellow fought for appearances, and down he went. The Gods favour one of two parties. Prince Turnus was a noble youth ; but he had not Pallas at his elbow. Ripton was a capital boy; he had no science. He could not prove he was not a fool! When one comes to think of it, Ripton did choose the only possible way, and we should all of us have considerable difficulty in proving the negative by any other. Ripton came on the unerring fist again and again; and if it was true, as he said in short colloquial gasps, that he required as much beating as an egg to be beaten thoroughly, a fortunate interruption alone saved our friend from resembling that substance. The boys heard summoning voices, and beheld Mr. Morton of Poer Hall and Austin Wentworth stepping towards them.

A truce was sounded, jackets were caught up, guns shouldered, and off they trotted in concert through the depths of the wood, not stopping till that and half a dozen fields and a larch plantation were well behind them.

When they halted to take breath, there was a mutual study of faces. Ripton's was much discoloured, and looked fiercer with its natural war-paint than the boy felt. Nevertheless, he squared up dauntlessly on the new ground, and Richard, whose wrath was appeased, could not refrain from asking him whether he had not really had enough.

" Never ! " shouts the noble enemy.

" Well, look here," said Richard, appealing to common sense, " I'm tired of knocking you down. I'll say you're not a fool, if you'll give me your hand."

Ripton demurred an instant to consult with honour who bade him catch at his chance.

He held out his hand. " There ! " and the boys grasped hands and were fast friends. Ripton had gained his point, and Richard decidedly had the best of it. So they were on equal ground. Both could claim a victory, which was all the better for their friendship.

Ripton washed his face and comforted his nose at a

brook, and was now ready to follow his friend wherever he chose to lead. They continued to beat about for birds. The birds on the Raynham estates were found singularly cunning, and repeatedly eluded the aim of these prime shots, so they pushed their expedition into the lands of their neighbours, in search of a stupider race, happily oblivious of the laws and conditions of trespass; unconscious, too, that they were poaching on the demesne of the notorious Farmer Blaize, the free-trade farmer under the shield of the Papworths, no worshipper of the Griffin between two Wheatsheaves; destined to be much allied with Richard's fortunes from beginning to end. Farmer Blaize hated poachers, and especially young chaps poaching, who did it mostly from impudence. He heard the audacious shots popping right and left, and going forth to have a glimpse at the intruders, and observing their size, swore he would teach my gentlemen a thing, lords or no lords.

Richard had brought down a beautiful cock-pheasant, and was exulting over it, when the farmer's portentous figure burst upon them, cracking an avenging horsewhip. His salute was ironical.

" Havin' good sport, gentlemen, are ye ? "

" Just bagged a splendid bird ! " radiant Richard informed him.

" Oh ! " Farmer Blaize gave an admonitory flick of the whip.

" Just let me clap eye on 't, then."

" Say, please," interposed Ripton, who was not blind to doubtful aspects.

Farmer Blaize threw up his chin, and grinned grimly.

" Please to you, sir ? Why, my chap, you looks as if ye didn't much mind what come t' yer nose, I reckon. You looks an old poacher, you do. Tall ye what 'tis ! " He changed his banter to business, " That bird's mine ! Now you jest hand him over, and sheer off, you dam young scoundrels! I know ye!" And he became exceedingly opprobrious, and uttered contempt of the name of Feverel.

Richard opened his eyes.

" If you wants to be horsewhipped, you'll stay where y' are!" continued the farmer. " Giles Blaize never stands nonsense!"

" Then we'll stay," quoth Richard.

" Good! so be 't! If you will have 't, have 't, my men!"

As a preparatory measure, Farmer Blaize seized a wing of the bird, on which both boys flung themselves desperately, and secured it minus the pinion.

" That's your game," cried the farmer. " Here's a taste of horsewhip for ye. I never stands nonsense!" and sweetch went the mighty whip, well swayed. The boys tried to close with him. He kept his distance and lashed without mercy. Black blood was made by Farmer Blaize that day! The boys wriggled, in spite of themselves. It was like a relentless serpent coiling, and biting, and stinging their young veins to madness. Probably they felt the disgrace of the contortions they were made to go through more than the pain, but the pain was fierce, for the farmer laid about from a prac- tised arm, and did not consider that he had done enough till he was well breathed and his ruddy jowl inflamed. He paused, to receive the remainder of the cock-pheasant in his face.

" Take your beastly bird," cried Richard.

" Money, my lads, and interest," roared the farmer, lashing out again.

Shameful as it was to retreat, there was but that course open to them. They decided to surrender the field.

" Look! you big brute," Richard shook his gun, hoarse with passion, " I'd have shot you, if I'd been

loaded. Mind! if I come across you when I'm loaded,
you coward, I'll fire!"

The un-English nature of this threat exasperated
Farmer Blaize, and he pressed the pursuit in time to
bestow a few farewell stripes as they were escaping
tight-breeched into natural territory. At the hedge
they parleyed a minute, the farmer to inquire if they
had had a mortal good tanning and were satisfied, for
when they wanted a further instalment of the same
they were to come for it to Belthorpe Farm, and there
it was in pickle : the boys meantime exploding in men-
aces and threats of vengeance, on which the farmer
contemptuously turned his back. Ripton had already
stocked an armful of flints for the enjoyment of a little
skirmishing. Richard, however, knocked them all out,
saying, "No! Gentlemen don't fling stones ; leave
that to the blackguards."

"Just one shy at him!" pleaded Ripton, with his
eye on Farmer Blaize's broad mark, and his whole mind
drunken with a sudden revelation of the advantages of
light troops in opposition to heavies.

"No," said Richard imperatively, "no stones," and
marched briskly away. Ripton followed with a sigh.
His leader's magnanimity was wholly beyond him. A
good spanking mark at the farmer would have relieved
Master Ripton ; it would have done nothing to console
Richard Feverel for the ignominy he had been compelled
to submit to. Ripton was familiar with the rod, a
monster much despoiled of his terrors by intimacy.
Birch-fever was past with this boy. The horrible sense
of shame, self-loathing, universal hatred, impotent
vengeance, as if the spirit were steeped in abysmal
blackness, which comes upon a courageous and sensitive
youth condemned for the first time to taste this piece of
fleshly bitterness, and suffer what he feels is a defile-
ment, Ripton had weathered and forgotten. He was

seasoned wood, and took the world pretty wisely; not
reckless of castigation, as some boys become, nor over-
sensitive as to dishonour, as his friend and comrade
beside him was.

Richard's blood was poisoned. He had the fever on
him severely. He would not allow stone-flinging,
because it was a habit of his to discountenance it. Mere
gentlemanly considerations had scarce shielded Farmer
Blaize, and certain very ungentlemanly schemes were
coming to ghastly heads in the tumult of his brain;
rejected solely from their glaring impracticability even
to his young intelligence. A sweeping and consummate
vengeance for the indignity alone should satisfy him.
Something tremendous must be done, and done without delay. At one moment he thought of killing all
the farmer's cattle; next of killing him; challenging
him to single combat with the arms, and according to
the fashion of gentlemen. But the farmer was a coward;
he would refuse. Then he, Richard Feverel, would
stand by the farmer's bedside, and rouse him; rouse
him to fight with powder and ball in his own chamber,
in the cowardly midnight, where he might tremble, but
dare not refuse.

"Lord!" cried simple Ripton, while these hopeful
plots were raging in his comrade's brain, now sparkling
for immediate execution, and anon lapsing disdainfully
dark in their chances of fulfilment, "how I wish you'd
have let me notch him, Ricky! I'm a safe shot. I
never miss. I should feel quite jolly if I'd spanked
him once. We should have had the best of him at that
game. I say!" and a sharp thought drew Ripton's
ideas nearer home, "I wonder whether my nose is as
bad as he says! Where can I see myself?"

To these exclamations Richard was deaf, and he
trudged steadily forward, facing but one object.

After tearing through innumerable hedges, leaping

fences, jumping dykes, penetrating brambly copses, and getting dirty, ragged, and tired, Ripton awoke from his dream of Farmer Blaize and a blue nose to the vivid consciousness of hunger ; and this grew with the rapidity of light upon him, till in the course of another minute he was enduring the extremes of famine, and ventured to question his leader whither he was being conducted. Raynham was out of sight. They were a long way down the valley, miles from Lobourne, in a country of sour pools, yellow brooks, rank pasturage, desolate heath. Solitary cows were seen ; the smoke of a mud cottage ; a cart piled with peat ; a donkey grazing at leisure, oblivious of an unkind world ; geese by a horse-pond, gabbling as in the first loneliness of creation ; uncooked things that a famishing boy cannot possibly care for, and must despise. Ripton was in despair.

" Where *are* you going to ? " he inquired with a voice of the last time of asking, and halted resolutely.

Richard now broke his silence to reply, " Anywhere."

" Anywhere ! " Ripton took up the moody word. " But ain't you awfully hungry ? " he gasped vehemently, in a way that showed the total emptiness of his stomach.

" No," was Richard's brief response.

" Not hungry ! " Ripton's amazement lent him increased vehemence. " Why, you haven't had anything to eat since breakfast ! Not hungry ? I declare I'm starving. I feel such a gnawing I could eat dry bread and cheese ! "

Richard sneered : not for reasons that would have actuated a similar demonstration of the philosopher.

" Come," cried Ripton, " at all events, tell us where you're going to stop ? "

Richard faced about to make a querulous retort. The injured and hapless visage that met his eye disarmed him. The lad's nose, though not exactly of the dreaded hue, was really becoming discoloured. To upbraid him would be cruel. Richard lifted his head, surveyed the position, and exclaiming, " Here ! " dropped down on a withered bank, leaving Ripton to contemplate him as a puzzle whose every new move was a worse perplexity.

George Meredith (1828–1909).

From " The Ordeal of Richard Feverel," by permission of Messrs. Constable & Co., Ltd., London, and Messrs.
Charles Scribners' Sons, New York.

English Preparations for the Armada

A combination of curious circumstances, assisted by four and twenty miles of water, had protected England hitherto from sharing the miseries of the rest of Europe ; but the exemption in itself, provoking to the natural envy of the less fortunate, could not last for ever. Not a year had passed without a warning of an intended invasion, and the notice to prepare had not been thrown away.

Thirty years of peace were supposed abroad to have emasculated the once warlike English nation, and to have so enamoured the people of quiet that they had no longer energy to defend their own firesides. If their vigour was unimpaired it was held certainly that they must want skill and experience. Their peculiar weapon the long bow, though it had not yet become a toy for the playground, could no longer decide a battle in the face of muskets and cannon ; and ardent Catholic Europe expected confidently that in collision with the trained regiments of Spain or France, the English militia would break in pieces at the first encounter. On the sea they were acknowledged to be still dangerous. The English corsair was a name of terror wherever there were Catholic traders to be pillaged. English merchantmen in the Mediterranean defied, engaged, and defeated the royal galleys of Spain, though outmatched to twice their strength. The general impression however was that if the naval defences could be pierced, and a well-found army be thrown on shore in any part of the kingdom, the power of England would collapse in ruins. London itself was undefended; and there was not a fortress in the whole island which would delay an army for an hour.

It has been seen that the Prince of Parma knew better what the country was made of. Although the hundred beef-eaters at court constituted the only permanently existing force in the service of the government, yet English and Spanish soldiers had encountered in many a hard fight on the Antwerp dykes or in the open field, and man to man the Spaniards could claim no superiority. He had experienced at Sluys that their engineering skill was not contemptible. He knew perhaps, to use the language of a writer, who after his own people respected the Spaniards above all other nations in the world, that " the English had always been, and at that present were, a free people, such as in few or no other realms were to be found the like, by which freedom was maintained a valiant courage in that people." Flanders, France, and Ireland had been training schools where many thousands of Englishmen of all ranks had learnt the art as well as the practice of war, while for the last eight years the militia had been carefully trained in the use of the modern weapons. Volunteer military schools had been established all over the country, gentlemen who had served abroad drilling the sons of the knights and squires. Three hundred London merchants who had seen service took charge of the city corps, and the example it is likely was imitated in the other towns ; while along the coast the privateering trade had made lessons in fighting a part of the education of every high-spirited lad.

In this way for eight years all England had been in preparation for the day of trial. It had not been without danger, for the general military organization had been made a shield behind which the Catholic families had been invited to make ready for rebellion. But the recusants were known and marked ; though every able-bodied man was put in training, the custody of the arms was reserved for those who could be trusted ; while the Protestants had the essential advantage that only they could furnish experienced soldiers. The Catholic English who made war their profession were serving abroad in the armies of Parma or Guise.

Thus it was, that when the long-talked-of peril was at the doors, and the people were called on to take their harness to resist invasion, a hundred thousand men, well officered and appointed, were ready at a day's notice to fall into their companies, and move wherever they were wanted. In the uncertainty where the Spaniards would land they were left at their homes, but with their line of action accurately laid down. The musters of the midland counties, thirty thousand strong, were to form a separate army for the defence of the queen's person, and were directed to assemble on the first note of alarm between Windsor and Harrow. The rest were to gather to the point of danger. The coast companies had orders to fall back, wherever the enemy landed, removing the corn and cattle, and avoiding a battle till the force of the neighbouring counties joined them. Should the landing be, as was expected, in Suffolk, Kent, or Sussex, it was calculated that between thirty and forty thousand men could be thrown in their way before they could reach London, while twenty thousand would still remain to encounter Guise, should he attempt a diversion in Hampshire or Dorsetshire.

How far forces thus constituted could have held their ground against the veteran soldiers whom they would have encountered, is a question on which the Prince of Parma's modest opinion is entitled to respect. In saying that he would have to fight battle after battle, it is to be presumed that he expected to win the first and perhaps the second. He expected also that his victories, like those of Pyrrhus, would be dearly purchased, and was very far from confident of the ultimate result. It would turn, in human probability, on the action of the Catholics, about which there was still an uneasy uncertainty. Philip's claims on the succession had alienated those who were Catholics rather by descent than fanaticism; but there was still a party of unknown strength under the influence of the Jesuits, of which the Earl of Arundel was the political leader, who had forgotten their country in their creed.

Father Darbyshire, an English Jesuit at Paris, told an agent of Walsingham's, "wishing to gain him to the cause," that "there was a band of men in London, with an officer sworn to the King of Spain, who had served under Parma," who, when the Armada was in the Channel, and "all the forces were drawn to the coast to resist invasion," intended to rise, set fire to the city, force the Tower, and release Lord Arundel. The Catholic standard was then to be raised, and the faithful everywhere would take arms and join the Spaniards. Even if there was no general rebellion, there was a fear that advantage might be taken of the absence of the loyal part of the population from their homes to make local disturbances, which would recall them from the army, or render them unwilling to join their standards, for fear of what might happen in their absence; and orders had been given by the council to use the gallows

M

freely on the slightest sign of a disposition to create trouble.

It was not by land, however, either that the Spaniards most feared the English, or that English statesmen and officers most relied on the powers of the country to defend itself, if it was only allowed fair play. An Englishman writing from Lisbon in the heat of the preparations for the Armada, reported, " that he had talked to many of the people there. They confessed they feared England on the water, but not on the land. The English, they said, were better warriors than they on the seas. Their mariners and gunners were better, and they feared their fireworks." Their experience of Drake and Hawkins and their companions had made them modestly conscious of their own inferiority where numbers were in any way equal.

But a fleet was not like the militia, a thing which the country could extemporize out of its own resources. The sea towns and private adventurers could fit out merchantmen to fight effectively against an enemy of their own size and strength ; but the largest ship in England at this time belonging to a private owner did not exceed four hundred tons, and of vessels of that size there were not more than two or three sailing from any port in the country. The armed cruisers which had won so distinguished a name in both hemispheres were of the dimensions of the present schooner yachts in the Cowes squadron. Philip, as a paternal governor, had encouraged shipbuilding in Spain by grants from the crown. For every vessel which was constructed above three hundred tons' burden he allowed four ducats a ton ; for every vessel above five hundred he allowed six ducats a ton : half of his grant being a bonus from the crown, half a loan to be repaid at leisure. Elizabeth had been advised to imitate the example. But she had preferred to leave her subjects to their own enterprise,

nor had she cared herself to lead the way of improve-
ment. When her naval resources were all counted,
including vessels which had been built by her father
and sister, the entire English navy contained but thirteen ships above four hundred tons, and in the whole
fleet, including fifteen small cutters and pinnaces, there
were only thirty-eight vessels of all sorts and sizes carrying the queen's flag. She had extended to the dockyards the same hard thrift with which she had pared
down her expenses everywhere. One precaution only
she had taken on the other side, characteristic also of
herself. She had placed at the head of her naval adminis-
tration the fittest person in her dominions to manage
it—Sir John Hawkins—who, sea robber, corsair, slave
hunter, as he was, yet with scrupulous fidelity threw
his mind and his fortune into his charge. When the
moment of trial came, Hawkins sent her ships to sea
in such condition, hull, rigging, spars, and running rope,
that they had no match in the world either for speed,
safety, or endurance. In the small *Swallow*, which had
been built by King Henry, Lord Howard offered to sail
to Rio Janeiro in the wildest storm that could blow.

A few words in detail may be spared to the constitution of the fleet which was about to accomplish so splendid a service. In ordinary times, one or two second
class vessels alone were kept in commission, which discharged the duties very imperfectly of Channel police.
The navy did not exist as a profession. It was the
queen's policy to appear as little as possible in any work
that had to be done, and to leave it to privateers. When
officers were wanted, they were chosen from those who,
like Sir Francis Drake, had distinguished themselves as
adventurers. The crews were engaged by the week,
by the month, or for some special service. A commission was appointed in 1583 consisting of Burghley, Walsingham, Howard, Drake, and Frobisher, to examine

into the condition of ships and stores, and so to organize
the yards at Portsmouth and Chatham that a squadron
could be held ready for sea if suddenly called for. The
whole navy was then thoroughly overhauled and repaired.
The charges for its future maintenance were divided
into ordinary and extraordinary. The first covered
repairs of all kinds, wages of shipwrights, carpenters,
clerks, watchmen, and cost of timbers, ropes, anchors,
mooring cables, and other necessary dockyard expenses.
For all this the queen allowed four thousand pounds a
year. She thought the sum excessive, but it could not
be brought lower. The second, or extraordinary charges,
covered special expeditions, for which in every instance
a particular estimate was made by the council, with
the lighter cordage, canvas, provisions, and other perish-
able stores of which the consumption varied with the
nature and extent of the service. It included also the
building of wharves, sheds, and storehouses, and also
of new ships, of which it was then decided that one at
least must every year be added to the fleet. Construction of this kind was done by contract. The ships were
expected to last in good condition thirty years at least.
The *Bonaventura*, a vessel of six hundred tons, was
built in 1560. She was with Drake in his expedition
to the West Indies in 1586. She carried his flag at
Cadiz in 1587. She had been engaged in every service
of consequence which had been undertaken since the
queen's accession. She was caught in a gale in the
beginning of 1588 and ran on a sandbank at the mouth
of the Scheldt, when, to use Lord Howard's words, " it
was thought impossible, unless she had been made of
iron, that she should not have been severely injured if
not lost." She was got off " without a spoonful of
water in her well ", and after a hard life of twenty-eight
years, the admiral said " there was not in the world a
stronger ship."

The cost at which vessels of this kind were constructed indicates that although contractors did their work well, they were contented with moderate profits. The *Rainbow*, a ship of five hundred tons, was set afloat fit at all points for sea for two thousand one hundred pounds; the *Vanguard*, also of five hundred tons, for two thousand six hundred pounds—or, allowing for the difference in the value of money, about thirteen thousand and sixteen thousand pounds respectively.

The wages of an able seaman under Henry VIII had been sixpence a day, or calculated in meat, drink, and clothing, according to the prices at the beginning of the sixteenth century, equal to six shillings of our money. Out of this he found his own living. As the value of money began to fall with the introduction of bullion from America, the government altered the mode of payment, themselves supplying the ships' rations. In 1585 the sixpence tried by the same standard was worth but three shillings, and the sailor received in money six and eightpence a month, while of food " of good and seasonable victuals " his allowance for every flesh day, i.e. for every Sunday, Monday, Tuesday, and Thursday, was a pound of biscuit or a pound and a half of bread, a gallon of beer, and two pounds of meat—salt beef, fresh beef or mutton, as the case might be. On the three other days he had the same quantity of beer and biscuit with half a ling or a cod, and half a pound of butter or a pound of cheese. The diet was occasionally varied by substituting bacon for beef and mutton, reducing the salt fish and increasing the butter and cheese; in all cases however the beer and bread remaining constant. These allowances were never altered whatever might be the variation of price; the cost of each man's three daily meals ranging from fourpence to sevenpence, at which it had permanently settled by 1588. The pay had been raised three years before at

the intercession of Sir John Hawkins from six and eightpence a month to ten shillings. The increase however
cost nothing to the crown, a smaller crew better paid
being found to do more effective service. Hawkins
said he had observed that with higher wages men became
more healthy and self-respecting, " such as could make
shift for themselves and keep themselves clean, without
vermin."

At the recommendation of the committee of 1583,
five new ships had been added to the navy, larger than
any which were already afloat ; the *Ark* and the *Victory*
of eight hundred tons, the *Bear* and the *Elizabeth Jonas*
of nine hundred, and the *Triumph* of a thousand. The
four last named had not been commissioned before 1588.
They had been constructed upon a new principle introduced by Hawkins. The high sterns and forecastles
were lowered, the keels lengthened, and the lines made
finer and sharper. Old seamen shook their heads at
the innovation, and foretold the usual disasters. They
would be too crank, it was said, to carry sail. They
were fit only for smooth water, and would founder in
the heavy seas of the Atlantic. The queen having paid
dear for them, shrunk from experiments which might
show her to have countenanced an expensive folly, and
had preferred so far to keep them safe at their moorings
in the Medway.

This was the condition of the royal navy of England
when called on to face the most powerful fleet which
had existed from the beginning of time. The privateers
promised to be useful as auxiliaries. The great merchants in every port armed the best of their ships.
London provided thirty ; Southampton, Poole, Dart-
mouth, Plymouth, Barnstaple, and Bristol contributed
as they were able ; and English brigs and barques of
two hundred tons, which never went to sea without being
prepared to encounter pirates, were no contemptible

allies. Lord Howard of Effingham had also two ships
of his own. Hawkins had four or five. Drake had a
whole squadron, for the western privateers rallied of
themselves to the flag of their chosen hero. But it
was on the queen's ships that the brunt of the battle
would have to fall, and above the largest of them the
vast galleons and galleasses towered up like Flemish
dray-horses by the side of the light Arabian coursers.

The *Bonaventura*, the *Golden Lion*, the *Rainbow*, and
the *Dreadnought* had been with Drake at Cadiz, and on
Drake's return, contrary to the advice of Burghley, had
been paid off and dismantled. The dockyards had
suffered like every other department of the public service from the queen's determination to make peace.
The repairing work had fallen far into arrears; and in
September, 1587, when Philip sent orders to Santa Cruz
to sail, and bade Parma prepare for his immediate
arrival, there was not a vessel in the Channel carrying
the queen's flag larger than a pinnace. The ships were
lying half-rigged at Chatham, with neither crews nor
officers, and requiring all of them to be examined and
refitted before they could be sent to sea for a winter's
cruise. Several weeks at least would be consumed
before men in sufficient numbers could be collected and
arms and stores taken on board. The queen, in Leices-
ter's words, " was treating for peace disarmed "; and
had Santa Cruz been able to use the opportunity he
would have found his way to Margate Roads without
receiving or firing a shot. Burghley, who had believed
that, for this year at least, the danger had passed over,
was roused at the beginning of October from his dangerous security. The galleon which Drake had brought
home with him in August was sold with her cargo, and
the money turned to instant account. An embargo
was laid on the merchant-ships in the various ports,
and their crews were impressed for the queen's service.

Hawkins was directed to put the whole navy as rapidly as possible in condition for sea; and, on the 21st of December, instructions were sent to Howard of Effingham " to take the ships into the Channel to defend the realm against the Spaniards."

Just as in Spain the intended storming of the stronghold of heresy had stirred the crusading spirit, and the Castilian nobles had sent the best of their sons to the Armada, so when the call was sounded at last for the defence of England, it rung like a trumpet-note through manor-house and castle. The chief of the house of Howard was in the Tower, praying for the success of the servants of the pope ; but the admiral, as if to wipe the stain from the scutcheon, brought his son-in-law, Lord Sheffield, and one at least of the Duke of Norfolk's sons, to serve at his side. Lord Henry Seymour came too, and all the distinguished seamen, Hawkins, Frobisher, Palmer, Townsend, and numbers more, whose names were only less illustrious. Drake was already at Plymouth with his own squadron of privateers and the *Revenge*, a queen's ship which had been sent down to him. The common sailors who had volunteered " were as able a company as were ever seen "—ill found in apparel, and desiring, not unreasonably, a month's wages in advance to provide themselves, but otherwise the pride and flower of English mariners.

James Antony Froude (1818–1894).

From " The History of England."

A Glimpse of Nature

Gather a single blade of grass, and examine for a minute quietly its narrow sword-shaped strip of fluted green. Nothing, as it seems, there of notable goodness

or beauty. A very little strength and a very little tall-
ness, and a few delicate long lines meeting in a point,—
not a perfect point neither, but blunt and unfinished,
by no means a creditable or apparently much-cared-for
example of Nature's workmanship, made, only to be
trodden on to-day, and to-morrow to be cast into the
oven,—and a little pale and hollow stalk, feeble and
flaccid, leading down to the dull brown fibres of roots.
And yet, think of it well, and judge whether, of all the
gorgeous flowers that beam in summer air, and of all
strong and goodly trees, pleasant to the eyes, or good
for food,—stately palm and pine, strong ash and oak,
scented citron, burdened vine—there be any by man
so deeply loved, by God so highly graced, as that narrow
point of feeble green. And well does it fulfil its mission.
Consider what we owe merely to the meadow grass, to
the covering of the dark ground by that glorious enamel,
by the companies of those soft, and countless, and
peaceful spears. The fields! Follow forth but for a
little time the thoughts of all that we ought to recognize
in these words. All spring and summer is in them—
the walks by silent, scented paths—the rests in noon-
day heat,—the joy of herds and flocks,—the power of
all shepherd life and meditation,—the life of sunlight
upon the world falling in emerald streaks, and falling
in soft blue shadows where else it would have struck
upon the dark mould, or scorching dust. Pastures
beside the pacing brooks, soft banks and knolls of lowly
hills, thymy slopes of down, overlooked by the blue
line of lifted sea, crisp lawns, all dim with early dew,
or smooth in evening warmth of barred sunshine, dinted
by happy feet, and softening in their fall the sound of
loving voices,—all these are summed in those simple
words; and these are not all. We may not measure to
the full the depth of this heavenly gift in our own land,
though still as we think of it longer, the infinite of that

meadow sweetness, Shakespeare's peculiar joy, would
open on us more and more ; yet we have it but in part.
Go out in the springtime among the meadows that slope
from the shores of the Swiss lakes to the roots of their
lower mountains. There, mingled with the taller gen-
tians, and the white narcissus, the grass grows deep and
free ; and as you follow the winding mountain path,
beneath arching boughs, all veiled with blossom—paths
that for ever droop and rise over the green banks and
mounds sweeping down in scented undulation steep to
the blue water, studded here and there with new-mown
heaps filling all the air with fainter sweetness,—look up
towards the higher hills, where the waves of everlasting
green roll silently into their long inlets among the shadows
of the pines ; and we may perhaps at last know the
meaning of those quiet words of the 147th Psalm, " He
maketh grass to grow upon the mountains."

John Ruskin (1819–1900).

*From " Frondes Agrestes," by permission of the Ruskin Literary
Trustees, and of Messrs. Allen & Unwin, Ltd.*

The Character of Dogs

The civilization, the manners, and the morals of dog-
kind are to a great extent subordinated to those of his
ancestral master, man. This animal, in many ways so
superior, has accepted a position of inferiority, shares
the domestic life, and humours the caprices of the
tyrant. But the potentate, like the British in India,
pays small regard to the character of his willing client,
judges him with listless glances, and condemns him in
a byword. Listless have been the looks of his admirers,
who have exhausted idle terms of praise, and buried
the poor soul below exaggerations. And yet more idle

and, if possible, more unintelligent has been the attitude of his express detractors ; those who are very fond of dogs " but in their proper place " ; who say " poo' fellow, poo' fellow," and are themselves far poorer ; who whet the knife of the vivisectionist or heat his oven ; who are not ashamed to admire " the creature's instinct " ; and flying far beyond folly, have dared to resuscitate the theory of animal machines. The " dog's instinct " and the " automaton-dog," in this age of psychology and science, sound like strange anachronisms. An automaton he certainly is ; a machine working independently of his control, the heart, like the mill-wheel, keeping all in motion, and the consciousness, like a person shut in the mill garret, enjoying the view out of the window and shaken by the thunder of the stones ; an automaton in one corner of which a living spirit is confined : an automaton like man. Instinct again he certainly possesses. Inherited aptitudes are his, inherited frailties. Some things he at once views and understands, as though he were awakened from a sleep, as though he came " trailing clouds of glory." But with him, as with man, the field of instinct is limited ; its utterances are obscure and occasional ; and about the far larger part of life both the dog and his master must conduct their steps by deduction and observation.

The leading distinction between dog and man, after and perhaps before the different duration of their lives, is that the one can speak and that the other cannot. The absence of the power of speech confines the dog in the development of his intellect. It hinders him from many speculations, for words are the beginning of metaphysic. At the same blow it saves him from many superstitions, and his silence has won for him a higher name for virtue than his conduct justifies. The faults of the dog are many. He is vainer than man, singularly

greedy of notice, singularly intolerant of ridicule, suspicious like the deaf, jealous to the degree of frenzy,
and radically devoid of truth. The day of an intelligent small dog is passed in the manufacture and the
laborious communication of falsehood ; he lies with his
tail, he lies with his eye, he lies with his protesting
paw ; and when he rattles his dish or scratches at the
door his purpose is other than appears. But he has
some apology to offer for the vice. Many of the signs
which form his dialect have come to bear an arbitrary
meaning, clearly understood both by his master and
himself ; yet when a new want arises he must either
invent a new vehicle of meaning or wrest an old one to
a different purpose ; and this necessity frequently recurring must tend to lessen his idea of the sanctity of
symbols. Meanwhile the dog is clear in his own conscience, and draws, with a human nicety, the distinction
between formal and essential truth. Of his punning
perversions, his legitimate dexterity with symbols, he is
even vain ; but when he has told and been detected in
a lie, there is not a hair upon his body but confesses
guilt. To a dog of gentlemanly feeling theft and falsehood are disgraceful vices. The canine, like the human,
gentleman demands in his misdemeanours Montaigne's
" *je ne sais quoi de généreux.*" He is never more than
half ashamed of having barked or bitten ; and for those
faults into which he has been led by the desire to shine
before a lady of his race, he retains, even under physical
correction, a share of pride. But to be caught lying, if
he understands it, instantly uncurls his fleece.

Just as among dull observers he preserves a name for
truth, the dog has been credited with modesty. It is
amazing how the use of language blunts the faculties of
man—that because vain glory finds no vent in words,
creatures supplied with eyes have been unable to detect
a fault so gross and obvious. If a small spoiled dog

were suddenly to be endowed with speech, he would prate interminably, and still about himself ; when we had friends, we should be forced to lock him in a garret; and what with his whining jealousies and his foible for falsehood, in a year's time he would have gone far to weary out our love. I was about to compare him to Sir Willoughby Patterne, but the Patternes have a manlier sense of their own merits, and the parallel, besides, is ready. Hans Christian Andersen, as we behold him in his startling memoirs, thrilling from top to toe, with an excruciating vanity, and scouting even along the street for shadows of offence—here was the talking dog.

It is just this rage for consideration that has betrayed the dog into his satellite position as the friend of man. The cat, an animal of franker appetites, preserves his independence. But the dog, with one eye ever on the audience, has been wheedled into slavery, and praised and patted into the renunciation of his nature. Once he ceased hunting and became man's plate-licker, the Rubicon was crossed. Thenceforth he was a gentleman of leisure; and except the few whom we keep working, the whole race grew more and more self-conscious, mannered and affected. The number of things that a small dog does naturally is strangely small. Enjoying better spirits and not crushed under material cares, he is far more theatrical than average man. His whole life, if he be a dog of any pretension to gallantry, is spent in a vain show, and in the hot pursuit of admiration. Take out your puppy for a walk, and you will find the little ball of fur clumsy, stupid, bewildered, but natural. Let but a few months pass, and when you repeat the process you will find nature buried in convention. He will do nothing plainly ; but the simplest processes of our material life will all be bent into the forms of an elaborate and mysterious etiquette. Instinct, says the

fool, has awakened. But it is not so. Some dogs—
some, at the very least—if they be kept separate from
others, remain quite natural ; and these, when at length
they meet with a companion of experience, and have the
game explained to them, distinguish themselves by the
severity of their devotion to its rules. I wish I were
allowed to tell a story which would radiantly illuminate
the point ; but men, like dogs, have an elaborate and
mysterious etiquette. It is their bond of sympathy
that both are the children of convention.

The person, man or dog, who has a conscience is
eternally condemned to some degree of humbug ; the
sense of the law in their members fatally precipitates
either towards a frozen and affected bearing. And the
converse is true ; and in the elaborate and conscious
manners of the dog, moral opinions and the love of the
ideal stand confessed. To follow for ten minutes in the
street some swaggering, canine cavalier, is to receive a
lesson in dramatic art and the cultured conduct of the
body ; in every act and gesture you see him true to a
refined conception; and the dullest cur, beholding him,
pricks up his ear and proceeds to imitate and parody
that charming ease. For to be a high-mannered and
high-minded gentleman, careless, affable, and gay, is
the inborn pretension of the dog. The large dog, so
much lazier, so much more weighed upon with matter,
so majestic in repose, so beautiful in effort, is born with
the dramatic means to wholly represent the part. And
it is more pathetic and perhaps more instructive to consider the small dog in his conscientious and imperfect
efforts to outdo Sir Philip Sidney. For the ideal of the
dog is feudal and religious ; the ever-present polytheism,
the whip-bearing Olympus of mankind, rules them on the
one hand ; on the other, their singular difference of size
and strength among themselves effectually prevents the
appearance of the democratic notion. Or we might

more exactly compare their society to the curious spectacle presented by a school—ushers, monitors, and big
and little boys—qualified by one circumstance, the introduction of the other sex. In each, we should observe
a somewhat similar tension of manner, and somewhat
similar points of honour. In each the larger animal
keeps a contemptuous good humour ; in each the smaller
annoys him with wasp-like impudence, certain of practical immunity ; in each we shall find a double life producing double characters, and an excursive and noisy
heroism combined with a fair amount of practical
timidity. I have known dogs, and I have known school
heroes that, set aside the fur, could hardly have been
told apart ; and if we desire to understand the chivalry
of old, we must turn to the school playfields or the
dungheap where the dogs are trooping.

Woman, with the dog, has been long enfranchised.
Incessant massacre of female innocents has changed the
proportions of the sexes and perverted their relations.
Thus, when we regard the manners of the dog, we see
a romantic and monogamous animal, once perhaps as
delicate as the cat, at war with impossible conditions.
Man has much to answer for ; and the part he plays is
yet more damnable and parlous than Corin's in the eyes
of Touchstone. But his intervention has at least created
an imperial situation for the rare surviving ladies. In
that society they reign without a rival : conscious
queens ; and in the only instance of a canine wife-beater
that has ever fallen under my notice, the criminal was
somewhat excused by the circumstances of his story.
He is a little, very alert, well-bred, intelligent Skye, as
black as a hat, with a wet bramble for a nose and two
cairngorms for eyes. To the human observer, he is
decidedly well-looking ; but to the ladies of his race he
seems abhorrent. A thorough elaborate gentleman, of
the plume and sword-knot order, he was born with a

nice sense of gallantry to women. He took at their hands the most outrageous treatment ; I have heard him bleating like a sheep, I have seen him streaming blood, and his ear tattered like a regimental banner ; and yet he would scorn to make reprisals. Nay more, when a human lady upraised the contumelious whip against the very dame who had been so cruelly misusing him, my little great-heart gave but one hoarse cry and fell upon the tyrant tooth and nail. This is the tale of a soul's tragedy. After three years of unavailing chivalry, he suddenly, in one hour, threw off the yoke of obligation ; had he been Shakespeare he would then have written *Troilus and Cressida* to brand the offending sex ; but being only a little dog, he began to bite them. The surprise of the ladies whom he attacked indicated the monstrosity of his offence ; but he had fairly beaten off his better angel, fairly committed moral suicide ; for almost in the same hour, throwing aside the last rags of decency, he proceeded to attack the aged also. The fact is worth remark, showing, as it does, that ethical laws are common both to dogs and men ; and that with both a single deliberate violation of the conscience loosens all. " But while the lamp holds on to burn," says the paraphrase, " the greatest sinner may return." I have been cheered to see symptoms of effectual penitence in my sweet ruffian ; and by the handling that he accepted uncomplainingly the other day from an indignant fair one, I begin to hope the period of *Sturm und Drang* is closed.

All these little gentlemen are subtle casuists. The duty to the female dog is plain ; but where competing duties rise, down they will sit and study them out, like Jesuit confessors. I knew another little Skye, somewhat plain in manner and appearance, but a creature compact of amiability and solid wisdom. His family going abroad for a winter, he was received for that period by

an uncle in the same city. The winter over, his own
family home again, and his own house (of which he was
very proud) reopened, he found himself in a dilemma
between two conflicting duties of loyalty and gratitude.
His old friends were not to be neglected, but it seemed
hardly decent to desert the new. This was how he
solved the problem. Every morning, as soon as the
door was opened, off posted Coolin to his uncle's, visited
the children in the nursery, saluted the whole family,
and was back at home in time for breakfast and his bit
of fish. Nor was this done without a sacrifice on his
part, sharply felt; for he had to forego the particular
honour and jewel of his day—his morning's walk with
my father. And, perhaps from this cause, he gradually
wearied of and relaxed the practice, and at length returned entirely to his ancient habits. But the same
decision served him in another and more distressing
case of divided duty, which happened not long after.
He was not at all a kitchen dog, but the cook had
nursed him with unusual kindness during the distemper ;
and though he did not adore her as he adored my father
—although (born snob) he was critically conscious of her
position as " only a servant "—he still cherished for her
a special gratitude. Well, the cook left, and retired
some streets away to lodgings of her own ; and there
was Coolin in precisely the same situation with any
young gentleman who has had the inestimable benefit of
a faithful nurse. The canine conscience did not solve
the problem with a pound of tea at Christmas. No
longer content to pay a flying visit, it was the whole
forenoon that he dedicated to his solitary friend. And
so, day by day, he continued to comfort her solitude
until (for some reason which I could never understand
and cannot approve) he was kept locked up to break
him of the graceful habit. Here, it is not the similarity,
it is the difference, that is worthy of remark ; the clearly

N

marked degrees of gratitude and the proportional duration of his visits. Anything further removed from
instinct it were hard to fancy ; and one is even stirred
to a certain impatience with a character so destitute of
spontaneity, so passionless in justice, and so priggishly
obedient to the voice of reason.

There are not many dogs like this good Coolin, and
not many people. But the type is one well marked,
both in the human and the canine family. Gallantry
was not his aim, but a solid and somewhat oppressive
respectability. He was a sworn foe to the unusual and
the conspicuous, a praiser of the golden mean, a kind
of city uncle modified by Cheeryble. And as he was
precise and conscientious in all the steps of his own
blameless course, he looked for the same precision and
an even greater gravity in the bearing of his deity, my
father. It was no sinecure to be Coolin's idol : he was
exacting like a rigid parent, and at every sign of levity
in the man whom he respected, he announced loudly
the death of virtue and the proximate fall of the pillars
of the earth.

I have called him a snob ; but all dogs are so, though
in varying degrees. It is hard to follow their snobbery
among themselves ; for though I think we can perceive
distinctions of rank, we cannot grasp what is the criterion.
Thus in Edinburgh, in a good part of the town, there
were several distinct societies or clubs that met in the
morning to—the phrase is technical—to " rake the
backets " in a troop. A friend of mine, the master of
three dogs, was one day surprised to observe that they
had left one club and joined another ; but whether it
was a rise or a fall, and the result of an invitation or
an expulsion, was more than he could guess. And this
illustrates pointedly our ignorance of the real life of
dogs, their social ambitions and their social hierarchies.
At least, in their dealings with men they are not only

conscious of sex, but of the difference of station. And
that in the most snobbish manner : for the poor man's
dog is not offended by the notice of the rich, and keeps
all his ugly feeling for those poorer or more ragged than
his master. And again, for every station they have an
ideal of behaviour, to which the master, under pain of
derogation, will do wisely to conform. How often has
not a cold glance of an eye informed me that my dog
was disappointed ; and how much more gladly would
he not have taken a beating than to be thus wounded
in the seat of piety !

I knew one disrespectable dog. He was far liker a
cat ; cared little or nothing for men, with whom he
merely coexisted as we do with cattle, and was entirely
devoted to the art of poaching. A house would not
hold him, and to live in a town was what he refused.
He led, I believe, a life of troubled but genuine pleasure,
and perished beyond all question in a trap. But this
was an exception, a marked reversion to the ancestral
type ; like the hairy human infant. The true dog of
the nineteenth century, to judge by the remainder of my
fairly large acquaintance, is in love with respectability.
A street-dog was once adopted by a lady. While still
an Arab, he had done as Arabs do, gambolling in the
mud, charging into butchers' stalls, a cat-hunter, a sturdy
beggar, a common rogue and vagabond ; but with his
rise into society he laid aside these inconsistent pleasures. He stole no more, he hunted no more cats ; and
conscious of his collar, he ignored his old companions.
Yet the canine upper class was never brought to recognize the upstart, and from that hour, except for human
countenance, he was alone. Friendless, shorn of his
sports and the habits of a lifetime, he still lived in a
glory of happiness, content with his acquired respectability, and with no care but to support it solemnly.
Are we to condemn or praise this self-made dog ? We

praise his human brother. And thus to conquer vicious habits is as rare with dogs as with men. With the more part, for all their scruple-mongering and moral thought, the vices that are born with them remain invincible throughout ; and they live all their years, glorying in their virtues, but still the slaves of their defects. Thus the sage Coolin was a thief to the last ; among a thousand peccadilloes, a whole goose and a whole cold leg of mutton lay upon his conscience ; but Woggs,[1] whose soul's shipwreck in the matter of gallantry I have recounted above, has only twice been known to steal, and has often nobly conquered the temptation. The eighth is his favourite commandment. There is something painfully human in these unequal virtues and mortal frailties of the best. Still more painful is the bearing of those " stammering professors " in the house of sickness and under the terror of death. It is beyond a doubt to me that, somehow or other, the dog connects together, or confounds, the uneasiness of sickness and the consciousness of guilt. To the pains of the body he often adds the tortures of the conscience, and at these times his haggard protestations form, in regard to the human deathbed, a dreadful parody or parallel.

I once supposed that I had found an inverse relation between the double etiquette which dogs obey ; and that those who were most addicted to the showy street life among other dogs were less careful in the practice of home virtues for the tyrant man. But the female dog, that mass of carneying affectations, shines equally in either sphere ; rules her rough posse of attendant swains with unwearying tact and gusto ; and with her master and mistress pushes the arts of insinuation to their

---

[1] Walter, Watty, Woggy, Woggs, Wogg, and lastly Bogue ; under which last name he fell in battle some twelve months ago. Glory was his aim and he attained it ; for his icon, by the hand of Caldecott, now lies among the treasures of the nation.

crowning point. The attention of man and the regard of other dogs flatter (it would thus appear) the same sensibility ; but perhaps, if we could read the canine heart, they would be found to flatter it in very different degrees. Dogs live with man as courtiers round a monarch, steeped in the flattery of his notice and enriched with sinecures. To push their favour in this world of pickings and caresses is, perhaps, the business of their lives ; and their joys may lie outside. I am in despair at our persistent ignorance. I read in the lives of our companions the same processes of reason, the same antique and fatal conflicts of the right against the wrong, and of unbitted nature with too rigid custom ; I see them with our weaknesses, vain, false, inconstant against appetite, and with our one stalk of virtue, devoted to the dream of an ideal ; and yet, as they hurry by me on the street with tail in air, or come singly to solicit my regard, I must own the secret purport of their lives is still inscrutable to man. Is man the friend, or is he the patron only ? Have they indeed forgotten nature's voice ? or are those moments snatched from courtiership when they touch noses with the tinker's mongrel, the brief reward and pleasure of their artificial lives ? Doubtless, when man shares with his dog the toils of a profession and the pleasures of an art, as with the shepherd or the poacher, the affection warms and strengthens till it fills the soul. But doubtless, also, the masters are, in many cases, the object of a merely interested cultus, sitting aloft like Louis Quatorze, giving and receiving flattery and favour ; and the dogs, like the majority of men, have but foregone their true existence and become the dupes of their ambition.

Robert Louis Stevenson (1850–1894).

From " *Memories and Portraits,*" *by permission of Messrs. Chatto and Windus.*

An Interview

At six o'clock the next day, the whole body of men in the choir emerged from the tranter's door, and advanced with a firm step down the lane. This dignity of march gradually became obliterated as they went on, and by the time they reached the hill behind the vicarage, a faint resemblance to a flock of sheep might have been discerned in the venerable party. A word from the tranter, however, set them right again; and as they descended the hill, the regular tramp, tramp, tramp of the united feet was clearly audible from the vicarage garden. At the opening of the gate there was another short interval of irregular shuffling, caused by a rather peculiar habit the gate had, when swung open quickly, of striking against the bank and slamming back into the opener's face.

" Now keep step again, will ye ? " said the tranter solemnly. " It looks better, and more becomes the high class of errand which has brought us here." Thus they advanced to the door.

At Reuben's ring the more modest of the group turned aside, adjusted their hats, and looked critically at any shrub that happened to lie in the line of vision ; endeavouring thus to give any one who chanced to look out of the windows the impression that their request, whatever it was going to be, was rather a casual thought occurring whilst they were inspecting the vicar's shrubbery and grass-plot than a predetermined thing. The tranter, who, coming frequently to the vicarage with luggage, coals, firewood, etc., had none of the awe for its precincts that filled the breasts of most of the others, fixed his eyes with much strong feeling on the knocker during this interval of waiting. The knocker having no characteristic worthy of notice, he relinquished it for a knot in one of the door-panels, and studied the winding lines of the grain.

" O, sir, please, here's tranter Dewy, and old William Dewy, and young Richard Dewy, O, and all the quire too, sir, except the boys, a-come to see you ! " said Mr. Maybold's maid-servant to Mr. Maybold, the pupils of her eyes dilating like circles in a pond.

" All the choir ? " said the astonished vicar (who may be shortly described as a good-looking young man with courageous eyes, timid mouth, and neutral nose), looking fixedly at his parlour-maid after speaking, like a man who fancied he had seen her face before but couldn't recollect where.

" And they looks very firm, and tranter Dewy do turn neither to the right hand nor to the left, but looked quite straight and solemn with his mind made up ! "

" O, all the choir," repeated the vicar to himself, trying by that simple device to trot out his thoughts on what the choir could come for.

" Yes ; every man-jack of 'em, as I be alive ! " (The parlour-maid was rather local in manner, having in fact been raised in the same village.) " Really, sir, 'tis thoughted by many in town and country that——"

" Town and country !—Heavens, I had no idea that I was public property in this way ! " said the vicar, his face acquiring a hue somewhere between that of the rose and the peony. " Well, ' It is thought in town and country that——' "

" It is thought that you are going to get it hot and strong !—excusen my incivility, sir."

The vicar suddenly recalled to his recollection that he had long ago settled it to be decidedly a mistake to encourage his servant Jane in giving personal opinions. The servant Jane saw by the vicar's face that he suddenly recalled this fact to his mind ; and removing her forehead from the edge of the door, and rubbing away the indent that edge had made, vanished into the passage as Mr. Maybold remarked, "Show them in, Jane."

A few minutes later a shuffling and jostling (reduced to as refined a form as was compatible with the nature of shuffles and jostles) was heard in the passage ; then an earnest and prolonged wiping of shoes, conveying the notion that volumes of mud had to be removed ; but the roads being so clean that not a particle of dirt appeared on the choir's boots (those of all the elder members being newly oiled, and Dick's brightly polished), this wiping must be set down simply as a desire to show that these respectable men had no intention or wish to take a mean advantage of clean roads for curtailing proper ceremonies. Next there came a powerful whisper from the same quarter :

" Now stand stock-still there, my sonnies, one and all ! and don't make no noise ; and keep your backs close to the wall, that company may pass in and out easy if they want to without squeezing through ye : and we two be enough to go in." . . . The voice was the tranter's.

" I wish I could go in, too, and see the sight ! " said a reedy voice—that of Leaf.

" 'Tis a pity Leaf is so terrible silly, or else he might," another said.

" I never in my life seed a quire go into a study to have it out about the playing and singing," pleaded Leaf, " and I should like, too, to see it just once ! "

" Very well ; we'll let en come in," said the tranter feelingly. " You'll be like chips in porridge, Leaf— neither good nor hurt. All right, my sonny, come along " ; and immediately himself, old William, and Leaf appeared in the room.

" We've took the liberty to come and see ye, sir,"

said Reuben, letting his hat hang in his left hand, and touching with his right the brim of an imaginary one on his head. "We've come to see ye, sir, man and man, and no offence, I hope ? "

" None at all," said Mr. Maybold.

" This old aged man standing by my side is father ; William Dewy by name, sir."

" Yes ; I see it is," said the vicar, nodding aside to old William, who smiled.

" I thought ye mightn't know en without his bass-viol," said the tranter apologetically. " You see, he always wears his best clothes and his bass-viol a-Sundays, and it do make such a difference in a old man's look."

" And who's that young man ? " the vicar said.

" Tell the pa'son yer name," said the tranter, turning to Leaf, who stood with his elbows nailed back to a bookcase.

" Please, Thomas Leaf, your holiness ! " said Leaf, trembling.

" I hope you'll excuse his looks being so very thin," continued the tranter deprecatingly, turning to the vicar again. " But 'tisn't his fault, pore feller. He's rather silly by nater, and could never get fat ; though he's a excellent tribble, and so we keep him on."

" I never had no head, sir," said Leaf, eagerly grasping at this opportunity for being forgiven his existence.

" Ah, poor young man ! " said Mr. Maybold.

" Bless you, he don't mind it a bit, if you don't, sir," said the tranter assuringly. " Do ye, Leaf ? "

" Not I—not a morsel—hee, hee ! I was afeard it mightn't please your holiness, sir, that's all."

The tranter, finding Leaf get on so very well through his negative qualities, was tempted in a fit of generosity to advance him still higher, by giving him credit for positive ones. " He's very clever for a silly chap, good-now, sir. You never knowed a young feller keep his smock-frocks so clane ; very honest too. His ghastly looks is all there is against en, pore feller ; but we can't help our looks, you know, sir."

" True : we cannot. You live with your mother, I think, Leaf ? "

The tranter looked at Leaf to express that the most friendly assistant to his tongue could do no more for him now, and that he must be left to his own resources.

" Yes, sir : a widder, sir. Ah, if brother Jim had lived she'd have had a clever son to keep her without work ! "

" Indeed ! poor woman. Give her this half-crown. I'll call and see your mother."

" Say, ' Thank you, sir,' " the tranter whispered imperatively towards Leaf.

" Thank you, sir ! " said Leaf.

" That's it, then ; sit down, Leaf," said Mr. Maybold.

" Y-yes, sir ! "

The tranter cleared his throat after this accidental parenthesis about Leaf, rectified his bodily position, and began his speech.

" Mr. Mayble," he said, " I hope you'll excuse my common way, but I always like to look things in the face."

Reuben made a point of fixing this sentence in the vicar's mind by giving a smart nod at the conclusion of it, and then gazing hard out of the window.

Mr. Maybold and old William looked in the same direction, apparently under the impression that the things' faces alluded to were there visible.

" What I have been thinking "—the tranter implied by this use of the past tense that he was hardly so discourteous as to be positively thinking it then—" is that the quire ought to be gie'd a little time, and not done away wi' till Christmas, as a fair thing between man and man. And, Mr. Mayble, I hope you'll excuse my common way ? "

" I will, I will. Till Christmas," the vicar murmured, stretching the two words to a great length, as if the distance to Christmas might be measured in that way. " Well, I want you all to understand that I have no personal fault to find, and that I don't wish to change the church music in a forcible way, or in a way which should hurt the feelings of any parishioners. Why I have at last spoken definitely on the subject is that a player has been brought under—I may say pressed upon—my notice several times by one of the churchwardens. And as the organ I brought with me is here waiting " (pointing to a cabinet-organ standing in the study), " there is no reason for longer delay."

" We made a mistake I suppose then, sir ? But we understood the young lady didn't want to play particularly ? " The tranter arranged his countenance to signify that he did not want to be inquisitive in the least.

" No, nor did she. Nor did I definitely wish her to just yet ; for your playing is very good. But as I said, one of the churchwardens has been so anxious for a change, that as matters stand, I couldn't consistently refuse my consent."

Now for some reason or other, the vicar at this point seemed to have an idea that he had prevaricated ; and as an honest vicar, it was a thing he determined not to do. He corrected himself, blushing as he did so, though why he should blush was not known to Reuben.

" Understand me rightly," he said : " the church-

warden proposed it to me, but I had thought myself
of getting—Miss Day to play."

" Which churchwarden might that be who proposed
her, sir ?—excusing my common way." The tranter
intimated by his tone, that so far from being inquisitive he did not even wish to ask a single question.

" Mr. Shinar, I believe."

" Clk, my sonny !—beg your pardon, sir, that's only
a form of words of mine, sir, and slipped out accidental
—sir, he nourishes enmity against us for some reason
or another ; perhaps because we played rather hard
upon en Christmas night. I don't know, but 'tis certain-
sure that Mr. Shinar's rale love for music of a particular
kind isn't his reason. He've no more ear than that
chair. But let that pass."

" I don't think you should conclude that, because
Mr. Shinar wants a different music, he has any ill-feeling
for you. I myself, I must own, prefer organ-music to
any other, I consider it most proper, and feel justified
in endeavouring to introduce it ; but then, although
other music is better, I don't say yours is not good."

" Well then, Mr. Mayble, since death's to be, we'll
die like men any day you names (excusing my common
way)."

Mr. Maybold bowed his head.

" All we thought was, that for us old ancient singers
to be finished off quietly at no time in particular, as
now, in the Sundays after Easter, would seem rather
mean in the eyes of other parishes, sir. But if we fell
glorious with a bit of a flourish at Christmas, we should
have a respectable end, and not dwindle away at
some nameless paltry second-Sunday-after or Sunday-
next-before something, that's got no name of his
own."

" Yes, yes, that's reasonable ; I own it's reasonable."

"You see, Mr. Mayble, we've got—do I keep you inconveniently long, sir ? "

" No, no."

" We've got our feelings—father there especially, Mr. Mayble."

The tranter, in his eagerness to explain, had advanced his person to within six inches of the vicar's.

"Certainly, certainly ! " said Mr. Maybold, retreating a little for convenience of seeing. " You are all enthusiastic on the subject, and I am all the more gratified to find you so. A Laodicean lukewarmness is worse than wrongheadedness itself."

" Exactly, sir. In fact now, Mr. Mayble," Reuben continued, more impressively, and advancing a little closer still to the vicar, " father there is a perfect figure of wonder, in the way of being fond of music ! "

The vicar drew back a little farther, the tranter suddenly also standing back a foot or two, to throw open the view of his father, and pointing to him at the same time.

Old William moved uneasily in the large chair, and constructing a minute smile on the mere edge of his lips, for good-manners, said he was indeed very fond of tunes.

" Now, sir, you see exactly how it is," Reuben continued, appealing to Mr. Maybold's sense of justice by looking sideways into his eyes. The vicar seemed to see how it was so well, that the gratified tranter walked up to him again with even vehement eagerness, so that his waistcoat-buttons almost rubbed against the vicar's as he continued : " As to father, if you or I, or any man or woman of the present generation, at the time music is playing, was to shake your fist in father's face, as might be this way, and say, ' Don't you be delighted with that music ! ' "—the tranter went back to where Leaf was sitting, and held his fist so close to Leaf's face,

that the latter pressed his head back against the wall :
" All right, Leaf, my sonny, I won't hurt you ; 'tis
just to show my maning to Mr. Mayble.—As I was saying, if you or I, or any man, was to shake your fist in
father's face this way, and say, ' William, your life or
your music ! ' he'd say, ' My life ! ' Now that's father's
nater all over ; and you see, sir, it must hurt the feelings of a man of that kind, for him and his bass-viol to
be done away wi' neck and crop."

The tranter went back to the vicar's front, and looked
earnestly at a very minute point in his face.

" True, true, Dewy," Mr. Maybold answered, trying to withdraw his head and shoulders without moving his feet ; but finding this impracticable, edging back
another inch. These frequent retreats had at last
jammed Mr. Maybold between his easy-chair and the
edge of the table.

And at the moment of the announcement of the
choir, Mr. Maybold had just re-dipped the pen he was
using ; at their entry, instead of wiping it, he had laid
it on the table with the nib overhanging. At the last
retreat his coat-tails came in contact with the pen, and
down it rolled, first against the back of the chair ; thence
turning a summersault into the seat ; thence rolling to
the floor with a rattle.

The vicar stooped for his pen, and the tranter, wishing to show that, however great their ecclesiastical dif-
ferences, his mind was not so small as to let this affect
his social feelings, stooped also.

" And have you anything else you want to explain
to me, Dewy ? " said Mr. Maybold from under the
table.

" Nothing, sir. And, Mr. Mayble, you be not offended ?
I hope you see our desire is reason ? " said the tranter
from under the chair.

" Quite, quite ; and I shouldn't think of refusing

to listen to such a reasonable request," the vicar replied. Seeing that Reuben had secured the pen, he resumed his vertical position, and added, " You know, Dewy, it is often said how difficult a matter it is to act up to our convictions and please all parties. It may be said with equal truth, that it is difficult for a man of any appreciativeness to have convictions at all. Now in my case, I see right in you, and right in Shinar. I see that violins are good, and that an organ is good ; and when we introduce the organ it will not be that fiddles were bad, but that an organ was better. That you'll clearly understand, Dewy ? "

" I will ; and thank you very much for such feelings, sir. Piph-h-h-h ! How the blood do get into my head to be sure, whenever I quat down like that ! " said Reuben, having also risen to his feet, sticking the pen vertically in the inkstand and almost through the bottom, that it might not roll down again under any circumstances whatever.

Now the ancient body of minstrels in the passage felt their curiosity surging higher and higher as the minutes passed. Dick, not having much affection for this errand, soon grew tired, and went away in the direction of the school. Yet their sense of propriety would probably have restrained them from any attempt to discover what was going on in the study, had not the vicar's pen fallen to the floor. The conviction that the movement of chairs, etc., necessitated by the search, could only have been caused by the catastrophe of a bloody fight, overpowered all other considerations ; and they advanced to the door, which had only just fallen to. Thus, when Mr. Maybold raised his eyes after the stooping, he beheld glaring through the door Mr. Penny in full-length portraiture, Mail's face and shoulders above Mr. Penny's head, Spinks's forehead and eyes over Mail's crown, and a fractional part of Bowman's countenance under Spinks's arm—crescent-shaped portions of other heads and faces being visible behind these —the whole dozen and odd eyes bristling with eager inquiry.

Mr. Penny, as is the case with excitable bootmakers and men, on seeing the vicar look at him, and hearing no word spoken, thought it incumbent upon himself to say something of any kind. Nothing suggested itself till he had looked for about half a minute at the vicar.

" You'll excuse my naming it, sir," he said, regarding with much commiseration the mere surface of the vicar's face ; " but perhaps you don't know, sir, that your chin have bust out a-bleeding where you cut yourself a-shaving this morning, sir."

" Now, that was the stooping, depend upon't, Mr. Mayble," the tranter suggested, also looking with much interest at the vicar's chin. " Blood always will bust out again if you hang down the member that ha' been bleeding."

Old William raised his eyes and watched the vicar's bleeding chin likewise ; and Leaf advanced two or three paces from the bookcase, absorbed in the contemplation of the same phenomenon, with parted lips and delighted eyes.

" Dear me, dear me ! " said Mr. Maybold hastily, looking very red, and brushing his chin with his hand, then taking out his handkerchief and wiping the place.

" That's it, sir ; all right again now, 'a b'lieve—a mere nothing," said Mr. Penny. " A little bit of fur off your hat will stop it in a minute if it should bust out again."

" I'll let ye have a bit of fur off mine," said Reuben, to show his good feeling ; " my hat isn't so new as yours, sir, and 'twon't hurt mine a bit."

" No, no ; thank you, thank you," Mr. Maybold again nervously replied.

" 'Twas rather a deep cut seemingly, sir ? " said Reuben, thinking these the kindest and best remarks he could make.

" O, no ; not particularly."

" Well, sir, your hand will shake sometimes a-shaving, and just when it comes into your head that you may cut yourself, there's the blood."

" I have been revolving in my mind that question of the time at which we make the change," said Mr. Maybold, " and I know you'll meet me half-way. I think Christmas Day as much too late for me as the present time is too early for you. I suggest Michaelmas or thereabout as a convenient time for both parties ; for I think your objection to a Sunday which has no name is not one of any real weight."

" Very good, sir. I suppose martel men mustn't expect their own way entirely ; and I express in all our names that we'll make shift and be satisfied with what you say." The tranter touched the brim of his imaginary hat again, and all the choir did the same. "About Michaelmas, then, as far as you be concerned, sir, and then we make room for the next generation."

" About Michaelmas," said the vicar.

Thomas Hardy (born 1840).

From " Under the Greenwood Tree," by permission of
Messrs. Chatto and Windus.

From a Diary of Travel

Saturday, 11*th April,* 1914. We have just forded the Alpheus in a ferry-boat. Ponies and all came with many swear words. The country is too lovely for me

o

to describe—the young green and the blue and now the forded river, brown and blue in the sun. It is exquisitely beautiful. They are now embarking the rest of the ponies—such a job. One is always troublesome. It is all done now and they are starting. The way the men pole that boat against the flood is masterly. P. is just taking a photo, so you will see it. They utilize the current so cleverly. All this is intoxicating. It's very hot already but I carry my umbrella open.

Midday. We have halted here on the outskirts of a village to rest and lunch. Infinitely and picturesquely shoddy—a street, a little square and houses wandering up and down the clay hills. Arcadia—but a very fruitful and green corner of it. The same mountains we are to cross lie just beyond us. We must be a showy train. P.'s photos will show you. There are much more flowers than there were last time—anemones, purple iris ; the blue iris is almost over but there are some buds to come. I shall try to get some bulbs after lunch. Oh, it is heavenly out here. Lunch is ready, I believe. No rock plants here because no rocks. These hills are made of mud.

We've had lunch and have dug you with the utmost care and pains one of the little blue iris. I'll send a flower with this from Andritzena to-morrow. To-night we sleep in a monastery in the mountains where there won't be any post. It may be that Andritzena even won't furnish a post office. In that case I must wait till we reach Megalopolis. We see Bassae to-morrow. I expect to find more plants in the mountains and have a cigarette box on purpose for them.

Ponies are much easier to ride than mules. Not so shockingly abrupt in their movements. These clay hills covered with dark green scrub remind me of the background of Piero della Francesca's pictures. Lots of

Aleppo pines about ; but we have lunched under olive trees. We are to start again directly, so I'll stop until the next halt.

After we reached Griga, which was meant to be our stop where we were at four, Stamati the second decided to go further to an inn at Tripi, two hours more mountains. It proved my undoing, and I got very queer, couldn't enjoy the very beautiful though stony way, and had to lie down with aspirin directly we got in. I've dined since and got perfectly well again—but it was a bore. He did it because he wanted to have plenty of time for Bassae to-morrow, but I fear he is crowding too much in a day. I hate cracking up—but after I've had enough I find that I go very rapidly to pieces. It's age I expect—but I am very out of condition too, having had no exercise for just a year.

We are in Arcadia you know, and I expect the loveliest time of the year. For a time we got above the leaves and found the asphodel in bud, and crowds of anemones, blanda, pulsatilla, the red coronaria, and the purple and pink anulata—Adonis, white orchids, one stylosa iris, and a lot of things which I don't know, a little pink thing like calendrinia, which we found before. Such lovely views of shadowed mountains and green plains. Peeps of the Ionian sea, with a view of Zante in the cloudy distance. Cyllene is covered with snow, and Erymanthus too. Oh, it is beautiful. The cistus is in flower, and so are the mastic bushes, with dark crimson flowers close to the stalk. We have been through woods a great part of the way, up and down an awfully stony road—too stony to ride. It was the riding which tired me. I think it is more fatiguing than walking. This khan is exactly like Lada—just as primitive—with no windows except wooden shutters, and no conveniences of any sort. The cook produced a five-course dinner—excellent—but the wine is du pays, and exactly like turpentine. It beat me. But Stamati's crowning merit is to have produced tea when I was at my worst, really nearly fainting. I forgive him every-thing for that. Not bad tea at all, it saved my life. There's nothing to do but to go to bed. I can't shave, and don't know when I shall. If I can clean my teeth, I shall be lucky. We are so tired that we shall sleep, I am sure. God knows what bedfellows we may have. I hope to post this at Andritzena, but don't know whether I can.

12th April. Just had an adventure. I went up a mountain before we started and heard a cracking in a bush, and presently emerged a large, black tortoise ! He looked at me, and didn't like the look of it, so with infinite pains he curled himself round and broke through to the brushwood again.

This khan is built on a ledge of the mountain where a little stream runs down. There are four enormous flat-topt plane trees in front—one of them at least six foot through the trunk. They have been cut to be as flat as umbrellas, and are in tiny leaf, about as far out as yours in the square, I expect. But these planes seem to begin green rather than brown. Then down the hill are cypresses and figs, then it suddenly gets very deep to a river. The mountain opposite is wooded on the top and has a little village half-way up—about twenty houses.

It has been a most lovely ride of three hours over several rivers and down places which you would think had been waterfalls—but you know the kind of thing. The only difference is that there is much more water at this time of year, which makes it more charming. The woods are like Fairyland and the flowers exquisite, but not exorbitant as they are in Switzerland. None of your gentian blue fields or great, sulphur anemones. Very frugal, like all Greek beauty. We are still two

hours from Andritzena, and that is two from Bassae,
so we have six hours more work to do since we sleep
at Andritzena. It is piping hot in the plains, but we
are never on level ground for more than half an hour
at a time, and generally we pick up a breeze on the
hillside. The ferns are a sight to see. They are load-
ing the horses ; it is time to go.

Maurice Henry Hewlett (1861–1923).

*From " The Letters of Maurice Hewlett," by permission of
Messrs. Methuen and Co., Ltd.*

A Fight Against a Typhoon

Jukes was as ready a man as any half-dozen young
mates that may be caught by casting a net upon the
waters ; and though he had been somewhat taken
aback by the startling viciousness of the first squall, he
had pulled himself together on the instant, had called
out the hands and had rushed them along to secure
such openings about the deck as had not been already
battened down earlier in the evening. Shouting in his
fresh, stentorian voice, " Jump, boys, and bear a hand ! "
he led in the work, telling himself the while that he had
" just expected this."

But at the same time he was growing aware that
this was rather more than he had expected. From the
first stir of the air felt on his cheek the gale seemed to
take upon itself the accumulated impetus of an avalanche.
Heavy sprays enveloped the *Nan-Shan* from stem to
stern, and instantly in the midst of her regular rolling
she began to jerk and plunge as though she had gone
mad with fright.

Jukes thought, " This is no joke." While he was
exchanging explanatory yells with his captain, a sudden

lowering of the darkness came upon the night, falling
before their vision like something palpable. It was as
if the masked lights of the world had been turned down.
Jukes was uncritically glad to have his captain at hand.
It relieved him as though that man had, by simply
coming on deck, taken most of the gale's weight upon
his shoulders. Such is the prestige, the privilege, and
the burden of command.

Captain MacWhirr could expect no relief of that sort
from any one on earth. Such is the loneliness of command. He was trying to see, with that watchful manner of a seaman who stares into the wind's eye as if
into the eye of an adversary, to penetrate the hidden
intention and guess the aim and force of the thrust.
The strong wind swept at him out of a vast obscurity ;
he felt under his feet the uneasiness of his ship, and he
could not even discern the shadow of her shape. He
wished it were not so ; and very still he waited, feeling
stricken by a blind man's helplessness.

To be silent was natural to him, dark or shine. Jukes,
at his elbow, made himself heard yelling cheerily in the
gusts, " We must have got the worst of it at once, sir."
A faint burst of lightning quivered all round, as if flashed
into a cavern—into a black and secret chamber of the
sea, with a floor of foaming crests.

It unveiled for a sinister, fluttering moment a ragged
mass of clouds hanging low, the lurch of the long out-
lines of the ship, the black figures of men caught on
the bridge heads forward, as if petrified in the act of
butting. The darkness palpitated down upon all this,
and then the real thing came at last.

It was something formidable and swift, like the sudden smashing of a vial of wrath. It seemed to explode
all round the ship with an overpowering concussion
and a rush of great waters, as if an immense dam had
been blown up to windward. In an instant the men

lost touch of each other. This is the disintegrating
power of a great wind : it isolates one from one's kind.
An earthquake, a landslip, an avalanche, overtake a
man incidentally, as it were—without passion. A
furious gale attacks him like a personal enemy, tries to
grasp his limbs, fastens upon his mind, seeks to rout
his very spirit out of him.

Jukes was driven away from his commander. He
fancied himself whirled a great distance through the
air. Everything disappeared—even, for a moment, his
power of thinking ; but his hand had found one of the
rail-stanchions. His distress was by no means alleviated
by an inclination to disbelieve the reality of this experience. Though young, he had seen some bad weather,
and had never doubted his ability to imagine the worst ;
but this was so much beyond his powers of fancy that
it appeared incompatible with the existence of any ship
whatever. He would have been incredulous about himself in the same way, perhaps, had he not been so har-
assed by the necessity of exerting a wrestling effort
against a force trying to tear him away from his hold.
Moreover, the conviction of not being utterly destroyed
returned to him through the sensations of being half-
drowned, bestially shaken, and partly choked.

It seemed to him he remained there precariously
alone with the stanchion for a long, long time. The
rain poured on him, flowed, drove in sheets. He breathed
in gasps, and sometimes the water he swallowed was
fresh and sometimes it was salt. For the most part he
kept his eyes shut tight, as if suspecting his sight might
be destroyed in the immense flurry of the elements.
When he ventured to blink hastily, he derived some
moral support from the green gleam of the starboard
light shining feebly upon the flight of rain and sprays.
He was actually looking at it when its ray fell upon
the uprearing sea which put it out. He saw the head

of the wave topple over, adding the mite of its crash to the tremendous uproar raging around him, and almost at the same instant the stanchion was wrenched away from his embracing arms. After a crushing thump on his back he found himself suddenly afloat and borne upwards. His first irresistible notion was that the whole China Sea had climbed on the bridge. Then, more sanely, he concluded himself gone overboard. All the time he was being tossed, flung, and rolled in great volumes of water, he kept on repeating mentally, with the utmost precipitation, the words : " My God ! My God ! My God ! My God ! "

All at once, in a revolt of misery and despair, he formed the crazy resolution to get out of that. And he began to thresh about with his arms and legs. But as soon as he commenced his wretched struggles he discovered that he had become somehow mixed up with a face, an oilskin coat, somebody's boots. He clawed ferociously all these things in turn, lost them, found them again, lost them once more, and finally was himself caught in the firm clasp of a pair of stout arms. He returned the embrace closely round a thick solid body. He had found his captain.

They tumbled over and over, tightening their hug. Suddenly the water let them down with a brutal bang ; and, stranded against the side of the wheelhouse, out of breath and bruised, they were left to stagger up in the wind and hold on where they could.

Jukes came out of it rather horrified, as though he had escaped some unparalleled outrage directed at his feelings. It weakened his faith in himself. He started shouting aimlessly to the man he could feel near him in that fiendish blackness, " Is it you, sir ? Is it you, sir ? " till his temples seemed ready to burst. And he heard in answer a voice, as if crying far away, as if screaming to him fretfully from a very great distance,

the one word " Yes ! " Other seas swept again over
the bridge. He received them defencelessly right
over his bare head, with both his hands engaged in
holding.

The motion of the ship was extravagant. Her lurches
had an appalling helplessness : she pitched as if taking
a header into a void, and seemed to find a wall to hit
every time. When she rolled she fell on her side head-
long, and she would be righted back by such a demolish-
ing blow that Jukes felt her reeling as a clubbed man
reels before he collapses. The gale howled and scuffled
about gigantically in the darkness, as though the entire
world were one black gully. At certain moments the
air streamed against the ship as if sucked through a
tunnel with a concentrated solid force of impact that
seemed to lift her clean out of the water and keep her
up for an instant with only a quiver running through
her from end to end. And then she would begin her
tumbling again as if dropped back into a boiling caul-
dron. Jukes tried hard to compose his mind and judge
things coolly.

The sea, flattened down in the heavier gusts, would
uprise and overwhelm both ends of the *Nan-Shan* in
snowy rushes of foam, expanding wide, beyond both
rails, into the night. And on this dazzling sheet, spread
under the blackness of the clouds and emitting a bluish
glow, Captain MacWhirr could catch a desolate glimpse
of a few tiny specks black as ebony, the tops of the
hatches, the battened companions, the heads of the
covered winches, the foot of a mast. This was all he
could see of his ship. Her middle structure, covered
by the bridge which bore him, his mate, the closed
wheelhouse where a man was steering shut up with the
fear of being swept overboard together with the whole
thing in one great crash—her middle structure was like
a half-tide rock awash upon a coast. It was like an

outlying rock with the water boiling up, streaming over, pouring off, beating round—like a rock in the surf to which shipwrecked people cling before they let go— only it rose, it sank, it rolled continuously, without respite and rest, like a rock that should have miraculously struck adrift from a coast and gone wallowing upon the sea.

The *Nan-Shan* was being looted by the storm with a senseless, destructive fury : trysails torn out of the extra gaskets, double-lashed awnings blown away, bridge swept clean, weather-cloths burst, rails twisted, light-screens smashed—and two of the boats had gone already. They had gone unheard and unseen, melting, as it were, in the shock and smother of the wave. It was only later, when upon the white flash of another high sea hurling itself amidships, Jukes had a vision of two pairs of davits leaping black and empty out of the solid blackness, with one overhauled fall flying and an iron-bound block capering in the air, that he became aware of what had happened within about three yards of his back.

He poked his head forward, groping for the ear of his commander. His lips touched it—big, fleshy, very wet. He cried in an agitated tone, " Our boats are going now, sir."

And again he heard that voice, forced and ringing feebly, but with a penetrating effect of quietness in the enormous discord of noises, as if sent out from some remote spot of peace beyond the black wastes of the gale ; again he heard a man's voice—the frail and indomitable sound that can be made to carry an infinity of thought, resolution and purpose, that shall be pronouncing confident words on the last day, when heavens fall, and justice is done—again he heard it, and it was crying to him, as if from very, very far—" All right."

He thought he had not managed to make himself understood. " Our boats—I say boats—the boats, sir ! Two gone ! "

The same voice, within a foot of him, and yet so remote, yelled sensibly, " Can't be helped."

Captain MacWhirr had never turned his face, but Jukes caught some more words on the wind.

" What can—expect—when hammering through—such—— Bound to leave—something behind—stands to reason."

Watchfully Jukes listened for more. No more came. This was all Captain MacWhirr had to say ; and Jukes could picture to himself rather than see the broad squat back before him. An impenetrable obscurity pressed down upon the ghostly glimmers of the sea. A dull conviction seized upon Jukes that there was nothing to be done.

If the steering-gear did not give way, if the immense volumes of water did not burst the deck in or smash one of the hatches, if the engines did not give up, if way could be kept on the ship against this terrific wind, and she did not bury herself in one of these awful seas, of whose white crests alone, topping high above her bows, he could now and then get a sickening glimpse —then there was a chance of her coming out of it. Something within him seemed to turn over, bringing uppermost the feeling that the *Nan-Shan* was lost.

" She's done for," he said to himself, with a surprising mental agitation, as though he had discovered an unexpected meaning in this thought. One of these things was bound to happen. Nothing could be prevented now, and nothing could be remedied. The men on board did not count, and the ship could not last. This weather was too impossible.

Jukes felt an arm thrown heavily over his shoulders ; and to this overture he responded with great intelligence by catching hold of his captain round the waist.

They stood clasped thus in the blind night, bracing each other against the wind, cheek to cheek and lip to ear, in the manner of two hulks lashed stem to stern together.

And Jukes heard the voice of his commander hardly any louder than before, but nearer, as though, starting to march athwart the prodigious rush of the hurricane, it had approached him, bearing that strange effect of quietness like the serene glow of a halo.

" D'ye know where the hands got to ? " it asked, vigorous and evanescent at the same time, overcoming the strength of the wind, and swept away from Jukes instantly.

Jukes didn't know. They were all on the bridge when the real force of the hurricane struck the ship. He had no idea where they had crawled to. Under the circumstances they were nowhere, for all the use that could be made of them. Somehow the Captain's wish to know distressed Jukes.

" Want the hands, sir ? " he cried apprehensively

" Ought to know," asserted Captain MacWhirr. " Hold hard."

They held hard. An outburst of unchained fury, a vicious rush of the wind absolutely steadied the ship ; she rocked only, quick and light like a child's cradle, for a terrific moment of suspense, while the whole atmosphere, as it seemed, streamed furiously past her, roaring away from the tenebrous earth.

It suffocated them, and with eyes shut they tightened their grasp. What from the magnitude of the shock might have been a column of water running upright in the dark, butted against the ship, broke short, and fell on her bridge, crushingly, from on high, with a dead burying weight.

A flying fragment of that collapse, a mere splash, enveloped them in one swirl from their feet over their heads, filling violently their ears, mouths and nostrils with salt water. It knocked out their legs, wrenched in haste at their arms, seethed away swiftly under their chins; and opening their eyes, they saw the piled-up masses of foam dashing to and fro amongst what looked like the fragments of a ship. She had given way as if driven straight in. Their panting hearts yielded too before the tremendous blow ; and all at once she sprang up again to her desperate plunging, as if trying to scramble out from under the ruins.

The seas in the dark seemed to rush from all sides to keep her back where she might perish. There was hate in the way she was handled, and a ferocity in the blows that fell. She was like a living creature thrown to the rage of a mob : hustled terribly, struck at, borne up, flung down, leaped upon. Captain MacWhirr and Jukes kept hold of each other, deafened by the noise, gagged by the wind ; and the great physical tumult beating about their bodies, brought, like an unbridled display of passion, a profound trouble to their souls. One of these wild and appalling shrieks that are heard at times passing mysteriously overhead in the steady roar of a hurricane, swooped, as if borne on wings, upon the ship, and Jukes tried to outscream it.

" Will she live through this ? "

The cry was wrenched out of his breast. It was as unintentional as the birth of a thought in the head, and he heard nothing of it himself. It all became extinct at once—thought, intention, effort—and of his cry the inaudible vibration added to the tempest waves of the air.

He expected nothing from it. Nothing at all. For indeed what answer could be made ? But after a while he heard with amazement the frail and resisting voice in his ear, the dwarf sound, unconquered in the giant tumult.

"She may!"

Joseph Conrad (1857–1925).

From " Typhoon," by permission of Messrs. Wm. Heinemann, Ltd.